Complete Book of

CHESS OPENINGS

EVERYDAY HANDBOOKS
BARNES & NOBLE, Inc.

ABOUT THE AUTHOR

The late Fred Reinfeld was an editor of *Chess Review* and a master chess player; he was former champion of the Marshall and Manhattan Chess Clubs and a former New York State Champion. Here, Mr. Reinfeld had applied his vast knowledge of board strategy to chess openings and variations for the beginner and the experienced chess player. Mr. Reinfeld was the author of over 50 books on chess, seven of which are Everyday Handbooks: *First Book of Chess* (co-authored with Al Horowitz), *Improving Your Chess*, *How to Win Chess Games Quickly*, *Attack and Counterattack in Chess*, *Chess Strategy for Offense and Defense*, *1001 Ways to Checkmate*, and this volume.

Complete Book of

CHESS OPENINGS

combining *The Seventh Book of Chess*
and *The Eighth Book of Chess*

By **FRED REINFELD**

Barnes & Noble, Inc. • **New York, N. Y.**
PUBLISHERS • BOOKSELLERS • SINCE 1873

CONTENTS

INTRODUCTION

All chess players are agreed that the opening plays a vital role in determining the future course of play. Proper play in the opening will give you a promising game; weak opening play can ruin your prospects from the very beginning. Consequently you must know the best lines of play in the opening.

To supply this information is not easy. Opening manuals contain thousands of alternative variations with tens of thousands of annotations. Most readers shrink back appalled by this more than lifetime task and despairingly conclude that they can never master the openings.

The present book is based on a different, far more practical approach. What the average player needs is *orientation*. Here you are given a concise summary of what the opening is intended to achieve, and what it actually does achieve. Then you are shown the most characteristic variations—the ones that best illustrate the spirit of the opening. This practical approach has two valuable advantages—it guides you to an understanding of, and familiarity with, the basic opening lines; yet at the same time it leaves you a lot of scope for your own initiative and desire to experiment.

You will also find this book a useful source of ready reference when you want information on one of the popular openings, or when you want to refresh or brush up on your knowledge of these openings.

Pages 6-61 deal with the Double King Pawn Openings, those in which White plays 1 P—K4 and Black replies 1 . . . P—K4. Pages 62-92 cover the Single King Pawn Openings, those in which White plays 1 P—K4 and Black makes a reply other than 1 . . . P—K4.

Study of the Queen Pawn openings is one of the most valuable ways for any chess player to improve his skill. Yet, despite the fact that these openings have enjoyed great popularity in master chess for over sixty years, the ordinary chess player continues to have a definite aversion towards them; even fear is not too strong a term for the traditional attitude.

Why is this?

The Queen Pawn Openings — those which start with 1 P—Q4 — are "close" openings. This means that the tactical contact between the opposing forces develops very slowly. There is room for a great deal of maneuvering, and it takes time to come to grips in fierce hand-to-hand fighting with the enemy. (As a matter of fact, this generalization does not always hold true. In the Albin Counter Gambit, for example, the emphasis is on attack and counterattack from the very start. Again, in such openings as the Nimzoindian Defense and the Gruenfeld Defense, victory will almost invariably go to the more aggressive player.)

Perhaps the average player is intimidated by the fact that these openings put a heavy premium on foresight and planning. Positional chess is of the essence here.

The present book has been written with a view to freeing the average player from these uncomfortable feelings. In every case you can get a general idea of the likely trend of the middle game. The long-term possibilities of the most important variations are carefully evaluated. Thus you know what to look for; you can foresee what aims must logically be pursued by both sides; the guiding themes of the middle game will no longer be a mystery.

All this is of the greatest practical value for this reason: since most players shun the Queen Pawn openings, the player who *is* familiar with them has an enormous advantage over most of his opponents. Players of every degree of strength are much encouraged when they start off with an opening advantage, and correspondingly downcast when they find themselves at a loss after the first few moves.

At the end of this book you will find several openings which do not come under the head of "Queen Pawn Openings." They have been included here in order to furnish a complete treatment of all the major openings.

CHESS NOTATION

As indicated in the following diagram, all the squares on the chessboard are *numbered* from both sides of the board; White's KR1, for example, is Black's KR8. Each square is also *named* for the piece occupying the file. Below the diagram is a list of the chief abbreviations used in chess notation.

BLACK

QR1 QR8	QN1 QN8	QB1 QB8	Q1 Q8	K1 K8	KB1 KB8	KN1 KN8	KR1 KR8
QR2 QR7	QN2 QN7	QB2 QB7	Q2 Q7	K2 K7	KB2 KB7	KN2 KN7	KR2 KR7
QR3 QR6	QN3 QN6	QB3 QB6	Q3 Q6	K3 K6	KB3 KB6	KN3 KN6	KR3 KR6
QR4 QR5	QN4 QN5	QB4 QB5	Q4 Q5	K4 K5	KB4 KB5	KN4 KN5	KR4 KR5
QR5 QR4	QN5 QN4	QB5 QB4	Q5 Q4	K5 K4	KB5 KB4	KN5 KN4	KR5 KR4
QR6 QR3	QN6 QN3	QB6 QB3	Q6 Q3	K6 K3	KB6 KB3	KN6 KN3	KR6 KR3
QR7 QR2	QN7 QN2	QB7 QB2	Q7 Q2	K7 K2	KB7 KB2	KN7 KN2	KR7 KR2
QR8 QR1	QN8 QN1	QB8 QB1	Q8 Q1	K8 K1	KB8 KB1	KN8 KN1	KR8 KR1

WHITE

King — K   check — ch

Queen — Q   discovered check — dis ch

Rook — R   double check — dbl ch

Bishop — B   en passant — e.p.

Knight — N   good move — !

Pawn — P   very good move — ! !

captures — x   outstanding move — ! ! !

to — —   bad move — ?

CENTER GAME

White's game is discredited from the very start by his premature development of the Queen. This enables Black to seize the initiative at move 3 by counterattacking against the White Queen. *Not recommended for White.*

WHITE	BLACK		WHITE	BLACK
1 P—K4	P—K4		2 P—Q4	PxP
3 QxP	N—QB3			

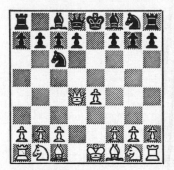

1

(Position after 3 ... N—QB3)

Black's gain of time enables him to take the lead in development.

4 Q—K3	N—B3

An amusing sample of White's difficulties is: 5 B—B4, N—K4; 6 B—N3, B—N5ch; 7 P—QB3?, B—B4!; 8 Q—N3??, BxPch!! and Black wins the Queen by a Knight fork.

5 N—QB3	B—N5

Another way is 5 . . . B—K2; 6 B—Q2, P—Q4; 7 PxP, NxP; 8 NxN, QxN and Black's game is decidedly freer.

6 B—Q2	Castles		7 Castles	R—K1

2

(Position after 7 . . . R—K1)

White's most likely move is 8 Q—N3 or 8 B—B4.

If White tries 8 B—B4 now, Black can win a Pawn with 8 . . . BxN; 9 BxB, NxP (not 9 . . . RxP??; 10 BxN! winning).

But then White has fairly good attacking prospects after 10 Q—B4, N—B3; 11 N—B3, P—Q3; 12 N—N5, B—K3; 13 B—Q3.

Therefore Black answers 8 B—B4 by 8 . . . N—QR4!; 9 B—Q3, P—Q4! with a fine initiative. This explains White's Pawn sacrifice on the next move:

| 8 Q—N3!? | NxP | 10 B—KB4 | Q—B3! |
| 9 NxN | RxN | 11 N—R3 | . . . . |

If 11 BxP?, P—Q3!; 12 BxP, Q—R3ch!; 13 K—N1, BxB; 14 QxB, QxQ and wins.

| 11 . . . . | P—Q3 | 12 B—Q3 | R—K1 |

Black is a Pawn ahead with a perfectly safe game. (He can also try the more complicated 12 . . . N—Q5!; 13 B—K3, R—N5; 14 BxN, RxB; 15 P—QB3, BxP!; 16 PxB, R—KN5; 17 Q—K3, QxPch; 18 B—B2, QxQch; 19 PxQ, RxP with a won ending thanks to his four Pawns for the piece.)

DANISH GAMBIT

This dashing attempt to seize the attack by sacrificing two Pawns can yield White a very powerful attack if Black does not defend carefully. However, as you will see, Black has several satisfactory defenses. Consequently, the Danish should be ventured only against weak opponents.

WHITE	BLACK		WHITE	BLACK
1 P—K4	P—K4		2 P—Q4	PxP
3 P—QB3			....	

3

(Position after 3 P—QB3)

Black's simplest course is now 3 ... P—Q4!; 4 KPxP, N—KB3!; 5 P—QB4, P—B4 (or even 5 ... P—B3!) with an excellent game.

3	PxP		4 B—QB4	....

If White decides to sacrifice only one Pawn by 4 NxP, Black is safe enough after 4 . . . P—Q3; 5 B—QB4, N—QB3.

Black has nothing to fear from 6 Q—N3 because of 6 . . . N—K4! Somewhat more troublesome for him is 6 N—B3, B—K3!: 7 BxB, PxB; 8 Q—N3, Q—B1; 9 N—KN5, N—Q1; 10 P—B4, B—K2; 11 Castles, BxN; 12 PxB, N—K2; 13 B—K3, N—B2; 14 R—B2, Castles; 15 QR—KB1, N—N3! Black is still a bit uncomfortable, but the extra Pawn must tell in his favor.

4	PxP	5 BxNP	....

The classic position of the Danish Gambit.

Even simplifying and returning the extra material may not give Black a safe game: 5 . . . P—Q4; 6 BxQP, N—KB3; 7 BxPch!, KxB; 8 QxQ, B—N5ch; 9 Q—Q2, BxQch; 10 NxB, P—B4; 11 KN—B3, B—K3; 12 N—N5ch, K—K2; 13 NxB, KxN; 14 P—B4. White will castle Queen-side and advance his formidable mass of King-side Pawns. Black is in trouble.

5	P—QB3!	7 N—B3	N—Q2
6 N—QB3	P—Q3	8 Castles	N—B4

4

(Position after 8 . . . N—B4)

Black's position, though somewhat cramped, is unassailable. After . . . B—K3 he can catch.up in development, and eventually his two extra Pawns must win for him.

BISHOP'S OPENING

This opening is considered inferior because it allows Black to seize the initiative by playing 2 . . . N—KB3 with counter-attack. However, Black must be on the alert for *transpositions* into other openings that may produce an unpleasant surprise.

WHITE	BLACK		WHITE	BLACK
1 P—K4	P—K4		2 B—B4	N—KB3

5

(Position after 2 . . . N—KB3)

White's colorless second move has enabled Black to take the offensive. White can try 3 N—QB3, transposing into the Vienna Game, page 12.

3 P—Q3	P—B3

Continuing his aggressive policy by preparing . . . P—Q4. (If 3 . . . B—B4; 4 P—B4 transposes into the King's Gambit Declined, page 20.)

Should White try to seize the initiative with 4 P—B4, there follows 4 . . . PxP; 5 BxP, P—Q4!; 6 PxP, NxP with a fine game for Black.

And on 4 Q—K2 Black gets a splendid attack at the cost of a Pawn: 4 . . . B—K2; 5 P—B4, P—Q4!; 6 KPxP (6 BPxP, NxP! is also good for Black), KPxP; 7 PxP, NxP; 8 BxP, Castles; 9 N—QB3, N—Q5; 10 Q—Q2 and now Black has 10 . . . B—QN5 with an excellent game—or 10 . . . P—QR3; 11 KN—K2, P—QN4; 12 NxN, QxN; 13 B—QN3, B—QN5; 14 Castles QR, P—QR4! with a winning attack.

4 N—KB3   P—Q4!

Black has an unbearably cramped game after 4 . . . P—Q3?

| 5 PxP | PxP | 6 B—N3 | .... |

6

(Position after 6 B—N3)

The subtle point of Black's play is that after 6 . . . B—N5ch! White cannot interpose 7 N—B3? because of 7 . . . P—Q5!

6	B—N5ch!		9 P—Q4	P—K5
7 P—B3	B—Q3		10 N—K5	N—B3
8 B—N5	B—K3		11 NxN	....

If 11 P—KR4, P—KR3!; 12 B—KR4, P—KN4!; 13 PxP, BxN; 14 PxB, N—KN5! with a powerful game for Black.

| 11 .... | PxN | 12 P—B3 | .... |

After 12 Castles, Black escapes from the pin with 12 . . . Q—B2!

| 12 .... | P—KR3 | 13 B—KR4 | .... |

Not 13 BxN, QxB; 14 PxP?, Q—R5ch etc.

| 13 .... | P—N4 | 14 B—KB2 | PxP |
| | 15 QxP | N—K5 | |

Black's position is more aggressive, and therefore more promising.

As in the Bishop's Opening, White gives Black a chance to counterattack with 2 . . . N—KB3. The struggle for control of the center is a very lively one. This opening always leads to interesting play because of the sharp clash of ideas.

(a)   3 P—B4 Variation

WHITE	BLACK		WHITE	BLACK
1 P—K4	P—K4		3 P—B4	P—Q4
2 N—QB3	N—KB3		4 BPxP	NxP

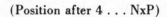

7

(Position after 4 . . . NxP)

If now 5 Q—B3, N—QB3!; 6 B—N5 (not 6 NxN?, N—Q5!; 7 Q—Q3, PxN; 8 QxP, B—KB4!), NxN; 7 NPxN, Q—R5ch; 8 P—N3, Q—K5ch with a favorable endgame for Black.

WHITE	BLACK		WHITE	BLACK
5 N—B3	B—K2		7 B—Q3	P—KB4!
6 P—Q4	Castles		8 PxP e.p.	BxP!

If now 9 Castles, N—B3 and Black maintains material equality. Nor can White capture twice on his King 4 without losing a piece. *The position is even.*

(b)   3 B—B4 Variation

WHITE	BLACK		WHITE	BLACK
1 P—K4	P—K4		2 N—QB3	N—KB3
	3 B—B4		NxP!?	

Leads to wild and woolly chess. A quieter and perfectly satisfactory alternative is 3 . . . N—B3; 4 P—Q3, N—QR4; 5 B—N3, NxB; 6 RPxN, B—N5 etc.

4 Q—R5   . . . .

Threatens mate. The tame 4 NxN is good for Black (4 . . . P—Q4! etc.).

| 4 . . . . | N—Q3 | 5 B—N3 | N—B3 |

So far so good, but now White again threatens mate, forcing Black to give up the Exchange.

6 N—N5!?	P—KN3	8 Q—Q5	Q—K2
7 Q—B3	P—B4	9 NxPch	K—Q1
	10 NxR	P—N3	

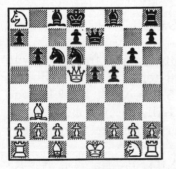

8

(Position after 10 . . . P—N3)

A very unclear situation, despite all the analysis that has been lavished on it.

After 11 P—Q3, B—QN2; 12 P—KR4, P—B5! (stops B—N5) Black has a powerful attack for his minus material. Thus, if 13 Q—B3, N—Q5; 14 Q—R3, B—KR3; 15 B—Q2, P—K5 *with a winning game for Black.*

On the other hand, after 11 N—K2!, B—QN2; 12 Q—B3, N—Q5; 13 NxN!, BxQ; 14 NxB, *White's material advantage should win for him.*

One thing is certain: White's repeated Queen moves leave him with a dangerously retarded development.

KING'S GAMBIT

This is the classic attacking line in the King Pawn openings. White offers a Pawn early in the opening in order to obtain a powerful Pawn center and an attack via the King Bishop file. Superior development for White generally gives him a winning attack. Superior development for Black generally gives him a winning defense.

(*a*) King's Knight's Gambit with 3 . . . P—KN4

This is the oldest and most complicated form of the King's Gambit.

WHITE	BLACK		WHITE	BLACK
1 P—K4	P—K4		2 P—KB4	PxP
	3 N—KB3	P—KN4		

Black's idea is to guard the Gambit Pawn at his King Bishop 5.

White can try to break up the Black Pawn formation with 4 P—KR4, but Black has a good reply in 4 . . . P—N5 driving the Knight back. If then 5 N—N5?!, P—KR3 and White is forced to play 6 NxP (Allgaier Gambit), which leaves him with inadequate material for the Knight after 6 . . . KxN.

More reasonable, after 4 P—KR4, P—N5 is 5 N—K5 (Kieseritzky Gambit); but after 5 . . . N—KB3; 6 B—B4, P—Q4!; 7 PxP, B—N2; 8 P—Q4, N—R4! Black has a splendid game.

$$4 \text{ B—B4} \qquad \text{....}$$

Black must be wary hereabouts. The over-anxious 4 . . . P—KB3?? leads to disaster after 5 NxP!, PxN; 6 Q—R5ch, K—K2; 7 Q—B7ch, K—Q3; 8 Q—Q5ch, K—K2; 9 Q—K5 mate.

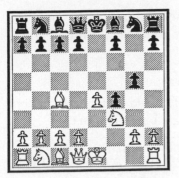

9

(Position after 4 B—B4)

White aims to develop quickly, while Black hopes to maintain his extra Pawn safely.

After 4 . . . P—N5 (too hasty); 5 Castles!?, PxN we have the famous Muzio Gambit. Then, after 6 QxP White has a magnificent development in return for his sacrificed piece. Black does well to avoid this hazardous line of play. Therefore:

4	B—N2	6 P—Q4	P—KR3
5 Castles	P—Q3	7 P—B3	N—QB3

10

(Position after 7 . . . N—QB3)

Black's sober development has given him a solid position which seems shatterproof.

8 P—KN3   . . . .

Logical: he tries to break up Black's Pawn-chain. Naturally Black does not oblige by replying 8 . . . PxP and thus opening the King Bishop file for White.

8 . . . .   B—R6!

By attacking White's Rook, Black gains time to complete his development. *The game is complicated, with approximately even chances.*

(b) King's Knight's Gambit with 3 . . . B—K2

This line and Variation *(c)* are favored by modern players as being simpler and less risky than Variation *(a)*.

WHITE	BLACK	WHITE	BLACK
1 P—K4	P—K4	2 P—KB4	PxP
3 N—KB3	B—K2		

There is more to this innocent-looking move than meets the eye, for if 4 P—Q4?, B—R5ch and White's King is forced to a bad square.

4 B—B4   . . . .

As usual, a developing move is best. If now 4 . . . B—R5ch; 5 K—B1 and White stands well despite the loss of castling. Black continues the policy of sound development with:

4 . . . .   N—KB3

If now 5 P—Q3, P—Q4! with an excellent game.

5 P—K5   N—N5!

11

(Position after 5 . . . N—N5!)

Black's advanced Knight is well placed. For example 6 N—B3, N—QB3; 7 P—Q4, P—Q3!; 8 P—KR3?, B—R5ch!; 9 K—B1, N—B7! and Black wins.

6 Castles   N—QB3

Also good is 6 . . . P—Q3; 7 PxP, QxP and Black has a fine development with nothing to fear.

7 P—Q4   P—Q4

If now 8 B—Q3, P—KN4! and Black stands well.

8 PxP e.p.   BxP   9 R—K1ch   N—K2
10 P—KR3   N—KB3

Black has a splendid position, and White still has the vexing problem of recovering the gambit Pawn.

(c) King's Knight's Gambit with 3 . . . P—Q4

WHITE	BLACK		WHITE	BLACK
1 P—K4	P—K4		3 N—KB3	P—Q4
2 P—KB4	PxP		4 PxP	N—KB3

White can now try to complicate matters with 5 B—N5ch, but Black simply replies 5 . . . P—B3, with a splendid game after 6 PxP, PxP; 7 B—B4, N—Q4!

For example 8 Q—K2ch, B—K2; 9 P—Q4, Castles; 10 BxN, PxB; 11 BxP, B—R3! Or 8 Castles, B—Q3; 9 Q—K2ch, B—K3 and Black has a fine game.

5 N—B3   NxP   6 NxN   QxN
7 P—Q4   . . . .

12

(Position after 7 P—Q4)

White hopes to regain his Pawn by 8 BxP, for if then 9 . . . Q—K5ch; 10 Q—K2 pins Black's Queen.

7 ....   B—K2!

This sound developing move indirectly guards the gambit Pawn, for if 8 BxP??, Q—K5ch wins the Bishop.

8 P—B4   Q—K5ch   9 K—B2   B—KB4
          10 P—B5   ....

With the powerful threat of 11 B—N5ch followed by 12 R—K1.

10 ....   N—B3!   11 B—N5   Q—Q4!

Prudently removing his Queen from the open King file.

12 BxP   Castles QR

13

(Position after 12 ... Castles QR)

Black has a fine game because of his pressure on White's weak Queen Pawn. If now 13 B—K3, B—B3! etc.

Black has escaped unscathed and has a fine game. A remarkable variation here is 13 B—K3, B—B3!; 14 Q—R4, B—K5! with this possibility: 15 BxN, QxB; 16 QxP, BxN; 17 PxB, BxP!; 18 BxB, RxB; 19 Q—R8ch, K—Q2; 20 QxR, QxQBP! and though Black is a Rook down, he has a winning attack!

(d) King's Bishop's Gambit

WHITE	BLACK		WHITE	BLACK
1 P—K4	P—K4		2 P—KB4	PxP
	3 B—B4		....	

14

(Position after 3 B—B4)

This opening is out of fashion as Black has easy counterplay with . . . N—KB3 and . . . P—Q4.

3 ....   N—KB3!   4 N—QB3   P—B3!

Preparing the counterthrust . . . P—Q4! If now 5 P—K5, P—Q4! with an aggressive game for Black.

         5 Q—B3   ....

Vainly trying to stop Black's next move. If instead 5 P—Q4, B—N5!; 6 Q—B3, P—Q4!; 7 PxP, Castles! and Black is well ahead in development.

5	P—Q4!	7 P—Q3	B—KN5
6 PxP	B—Q3	8 Q—B2	Castles

Black's marked lead in development gives him much the better game. A plausible continuation to emphasize this advantage is the following:

9 BxP	R—K1ch	12 QN—K2	NxP
10 K—B1	P—QN4	13 BxN	PxB
11 B—QN3	P—N5	14 Q—N3	BxNch
	15 NxB	Q—B3!	

Black wins, his chief threat being 16 . . . RxN!
The moral of all these variations is that if Black fosters his development carefully and avoids confusing complications, he remains with much the better game.

KING'S GAMBIT DECLINED

By refusing to accept the gambit, Black hopes to avoid prepared variations and dangerous attacks. In general, therefore, the play in this opening is less critical than in the gambit accepted.

(a) 4 B—B4 Variation

WHITE	BLACK		WHITE	BLACK
1 P—K4	P—K4		2 P—KB4	B—B4

The key move to the whole situation. If now 3 PxP??, Black has the crushing reply 3 . . . Q—R5ch forcing checkmate or winning a Rook.

3 N—KB3	P—Q3		5 N—B3	N—B3
4 B—B4	N—KB3		6 P—Q3	. . . .

15

(Position after 6 P—Q3)

Black can try the aggressive but risky course 6 . . . B—KN5; 7 N—QR4, BxN; 8 QxB, N—Q5; 9 Q—N3!? with highly complicated play. The following recommendation is safer and simpler by far.

6 . . . .   B—K3!

Even game. Black has nothing to fear after 7 BxB, PxB; while if 7 B—N5, P—QR3; 8 BxNch, PxB; 9 P—B5, B—B1

*he has two serviceable Bishops and the freeing move . . .
P—Q4.*

(b) 4 P—B3 Variation

WHITE	BLACK		WHITE	BLACK
1 P—K4	P—K4		3 N—KB3	P—Q3
2 P—KB4	B—B4		4 P—B3	....

16

(Position after 4 P—B3)

*White hopes to build a strong Pawn
center by continuing with P—Q4.
Black must counterattack precisely.*

4 ....   N—KB3!

Better than 4 . . . B—KN5; 5 PxP!, PxP; 6 Q—R4ch!,
B—Q2 (forced); 7 Q—B2 and White's game is freer.

Likewise after 4 . . . P—B4; 5 BPxP, QPxP; 6 P—Q4!,
KPxP; 7 B—QB4!, N—KB3; 8 P—K5, N—K5; 9 PxP,
B—N5ch; 10 B—Q2, BxBch; 11 QNxB, N—QB3; 12 P—Q5
Black's game is very difficult because White's center Pawn
position is so powerful.

5 PxP	PxP		8 P—K5	N—Q4
6 P—Q4	PxP		9 B—QB4	B—K3
7 PxP	B—N3!		10 Q—N3	Castles

*Even game, in view of the strong position of Black's Knight
at Queen 4. Though White's Pawn center looks formidable, it
may become weak later on after a well-timed . . . P—KB3.*

FALKBEER COUNTER GAMBIT

Counter gambits must be viewed with skepticism. It is generally doubtful that Black can snatch the initiative at an early stage. In this opening, for example, Black's policy of temporarily—and in some cases, permanently—sacrificing a Pawn, does not seem to be justified.

WHITE	BLACK		WHITE	BLACK
1 P—K4	P—K4		2 P—KB4	P—Q4
3 KPxP	P—K5			

17
(Position after 3 . . . P—K5)

This is the position Black aims for with his key second move. Black hopes to use his King Pawn as a stumbling block to White's development. Hence White's reply.

4 P—Q3   N—KB3

After 4 . . . PxP; 5 QxP, N—KB3; 6 N—QB3, B—QB4; 7 B—Q2, Castles; 8 Castles, Black has no compensation for the lost Pawn.

5 Q—K2!   . . . .

The pin on the King Pawn is very effective.

If instead 5 N—Q2 Black gets a good game with 5 . . . PxP; 6 BxP, NxP etc.

5	QxP	9 PxP!	QxKP
6 N—QB3	B—QN5	10 QxQch	NxQ
7 B—Q2	BxN	11 BxP	R—N1
8 BxB	B—N5	12 B—K5	N—QB3
	13 B—Q3	....	

White's extra Pawn gives him the advantage.

18

(Position after 13 B—Q3)

Black has no compensation for the Pawn minus.

There is another counter gambit—an early attempt by Black to wrest the initiative from White. As such, it is suspect. What makes this counter gambit all the more dubious is that it is foolishly adopted as a reply to what is undoubtedly White's strongest *developing* move, 2 N—KB3.

WHITE	BLACK		WHITE	BLACK
1 P—K4	P—K4		2 N—KB3	P—KB4

19

(Position after 2 . . . P—KB4)

Black's advance of the King Bishop Pawn is premature. It weakens Black's King's position and allows White to gain time with a formidable threat.

	3 NxP		. . . .

Threatening 4 Q—R5ch and if 4 . . . P—KN3; 5 NxNP. Hence Black's reply.

3	Q—B3		5 N—B4	PxP
4 P—Q4	P—Q3		6 N—B3	Q—N3

The tricky 6 . . . P—B3 does not work because of 7 NxP, Q—K3; 8 Q—K2, P—Q4; 9 N/K4—Q6ch, K—Q2; 10 N—B7!!

20

(Position after 6 . . ∴ Q—N3)

White is well ahead in development and Black's forces are split. His Queen will be sadly missed from the Queen-side.

| 7 B—B4 | N—KB3 | 8 N—K3 | B—K2 |

After 8 . . . B—K3; 9 P—Q5 followed by 10 Q—Q4, Black's game is disorganized and his King Pawn is weak.

| 9 B—B4 | P—B3 | 10 P—Q5! | . . . . |

White has definitely the better game because of his superior development. Black's King Pawn lacks the natural support of . . . P—Q4 and the prospects for development of his Queen-side forces remain bleak.

PHILIDOR'S DEFENSE

Black's passive second move immediately puts him on the defensive with a cramped and passive game. White has the initiative and much more freedom no matter how Black proceeds.

(a) 3 . . . PxP Variation

WHITE	BLACK		WHITE	BLACK
1 P—K4	P—K4		2 N—KB3	P—Q3

The characteristic move of this defense. Note that it hems in Black's King Bishop.

3 P—Q4	PxP

Black surrenders the center, giving White the opportunity to develop his Queen aggressively.

4 QxP!	N—QB3	7 N—B3	N—B3
5 B—QN5!	B—Q2	8 B—N5	B—K2
6 BxN	BxB	9 Castles QR	. . . .

21

(Position after 9 Castles QR)

White has a splendid initiative with a marked lead in development and plenty of room for his pieces.

(b) 3 . . . N—Q2 Variation

	WHITE	BLACK		WHITE	BLACK
1	P—K4	P—K4	3	P—Q4	N—Q2
2	N—KB3	P—Q3	4	B—QB4!	. . . .

By playing 3 . . . N—Q2 Black has announced his policy of not giving up the center as in the previous variation. However, his position is badly constricted.

22

(Position after 4 B—QB4!)

Black is in trouble. If now 4 . . . B—K2?; 5 PxP!, NxP; 6 NxN, PxN; 7 Q—R5 — or 5 . . . PxP?; 6 Q—Q5. In either case White wins material.

4	. . . .	P—QB3	6	Castles	KN—B3
5	N—B3	B—K2	7	P—QR4!	. . . .

Prevents Black from making some room for his pieces on the Queen-side with . . . P—QN4 etc.

White has distinctly the better game because his pieces have far more mobility. A likely continuation is 7 . . . Q—B2; 8 Q—K2, Castles; 9 B—R2 followed by B—K3 and White maintains a noticeably freer position.

On the surface this is an aggressive defense, as Black counterattacks on the second move. Actually White has several simplifying drawish possibilities. Consequently Black should avoid the Petroff *if he is out to win.* On the other hand, if White strives for the initiative, Black has just enough resources to hold the position.

WHITE	BLACK		WHITE	BLACK
1 P—K4	P—K4		2 N—KB3	N—KB3

The key move. If now 3 P—Q4, PxP!; 4 P—K5, N—K5; 5 QxP, P—Q4; 6 PxP e.p., NxQP with even chances.

3 NxP   ....

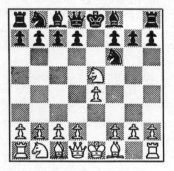

23

(Position after 3 NxP)

This position is not as harmless as it looks. If now 3 . . . NxP??; 4 Q—K2! and White forces the win of some material—for example 4 . . . N—KB3???; 5 N—B6 dis ch.

3	P—Q3!		4 N—KB3	NxP

Here White has a colorless line which spoils the Petroff for aggressive players: 5 Q—K2, Q—K2; 6 P—Q3, N—KB3; 7 B—N5 etc.

5 P—Q4	P—Q4		6 B—Q3	....

24

(Position after 6 B—Q3)

Momentarily it seems as if White may succeed in getting a slight initiative, say 6 . . . B—Q3; 7 Castles, Castles; 8 P—B4!, P—QB3; 9 N—B3 etc.

6	B—K2	7 Castles	N—QB3
8 P—B4	. . . .		

Again White seems to be making headway, for example 8 . . . N—B3; 9 P—B5! and Black's game is cramped.

8	N—QN5!	10 QxN	QxP
9 PxP	NxB	11 R—K1	B—KB4

Even game. A plausible follow-up is 12 N—B3, NxN; 13 QxN, P—QB3; 14 R—K5, Q—Q2; 15 P—Q5!, Castles KR!; 16 PxP, PxP. In that case Black's Queen-side Pawns have been weakened, but he has good Bishops.

SCOTCH GAME

With his third and fourth moves, White violates the principles of rapid development. At move 4, Black is able to develop with gain of time and is thus assured of equality.

(a) 4 . . . B—B4 Variation

WHITE	BLACK		WHITE	BLACK
1 P—K4	P—K4		3 P—Q4	PxP
2 N—KB3	N—QB3		4 NxP	. . . .

A possibility here is 4 B—QB4. After 4 . . . N—B3 White can lead into the Two Knights' Defense with 5 Castles or 5 P—K5 (pages 44-47), or he can continue the gambit proper with 5 P—B3, PxP; 6 NxP. This gives him an active development as partial compensation for his Pawn.

4	B—B4

25

(Position after 4 . . . B—B4)

Black develops with attack—pure gain of time. The following struggle for control of the center squares is very interesting and certainly offers Black no difficulty.

5 B—K3	Q—B3		8 NxB	Castles
6 P—QB3	KN—K2		9 B—K2	P—Q3
7 N—B2	BxB		10 Castles	B—K3
	11 N—Q2	P—Q4!		

The classic equalizing move. The game is perfectly even.

(b) 4 . . . N—B3 Variation

WHITE	BLACK		WHITE	BLACK
1 P—K4	P—K4		5 N—QB3	B—N5
2 N—KB3	N—QB3		6 NxN	NPxN
3 P—Q4	PxP		7 B—Q3	P—Q4
4 NxP	N—B3		8 PxP	. . . .

After 8 P—K5, Black gets a good game with 8 . . . N—N5 or 8 . . . N—K5.

26

(Position after 8 PxP)

Black's simplest equalizing method is 8 . . . Q—K2ch; 9 Q—K2, NxP; 10 QxQch, KxQ etc.

8	PxP		10 B—KN5	B—K3
9 Castles	Castles		11 Q—B3	B—K2

Even game. White's position is more aggressive, but Black has ample resources.

Whereas in the Scotch Game White advances too rapidly in the center to achieve any lasting effect, in the Ponziani Opening he advances too slowly. So Black equalizes without any trouble.

WHITE	BLACK		WHITE	BLACK
1 P—K4	P—K4		2 N—KB3	N—QB3
	3 P—B3		N—B3!	

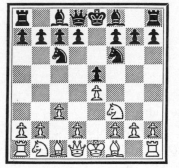

27

(Position after 3 . . . N—B3!)

White's third move holds up his development and takes away his Queen Knight's best square.

4 P—Q4	P—Q4!

Much better than 4 . . . NxKP?; 5 P—Q5, N—N1; 6 B—Q3!, N—B4; 7 NxP when Black has an unpromising position.

5 B—QN5!	. . . .

White wisely takes the prudent course. If 5 KPxP, QxP; 6 B—K2, P—K5; 7 KN—Q2, P—K6!; 8 PxP, QxNP Black has the initiative.

Meanwhile White hopes for some such continuation as 5 . . . QPxP; 6 NxP, which gives him fair prospects of initiative. In addition, even after 6 . . . B—Q2 White would permanently spoil Black's Queen-side Pawn position with 7 BxN etc.

5	....	KPxP	8 BxBch	QxB
6	NxP	B—Q2	9 QxN	QxP
7	PxP	NxN	10 Q—K3ch	B—K2

Black has a slight lead in development, but the position may be considered even.

HUNGARIAN DEFENSE

Black sometimes adopts this defense to evade the Giuoco Piano or Evans Gambit (pages 26, 42). However, the result is a cramped game for him. Therefore this defense is not recommended for Black.

WHITE	BLACK		WHITE	BLACK
1 P—K4	P—K4		2 N—KB3	N—QB3
	3 B—B4 .	B—K2		

Black's last move is the characteristic move of this defense.

4 P—Q4!   . . . .

28

(Position after 4 P—Q4!)

If Black plays 4 . . . PxP the sequel might be 5 NxP, P—Q3; 6 Castles, N—B3; 7 N—QB3, Castles; 8 P—KR3 when Black has a cramped position reminiscent of Philidor's Defense (page 26).

4	P—Q3		5 P—Q5!	. . . .

The key move of White's plan: Black is to be permanently tied up.

5	N—N1		6 B—Q3!	. . . .

White must prevent Black's only way of seeking freedom —by . . . P—KB4.

| 6 .... | N—KB3 | | 7 P—B4 | Castles |

Or 7 . . . QN—Q2; 8 N—B3, Castles; 9 P—KR3, N—B4;
10 B—B2, P—QR4; 11 B—K3 and Black's position is
crowded just as badly as in the text line.

8 P—KR3!	P—B3	10 B—K3	N—B2
9 N—B3	N—R3	11 Castles	KN—K1
	12 Q—B2!	....	

*White has much the better game. Black's position is sadly
constricted.*

This is the first opening in our survey which is based on strictly logical ideas. White strives for the initiative with his second move (2 N—KB3), and continues with 3 B—B4. Thus he gives his King Bishop an aggressive diagonal and attempts to restrain the liberating . . . P—Q4. Then he proceeds to construct a strong Pawn center.

All this sounds formidable, and it is. Black can easily go wrong if he does not know the safest lines.

(a) 4 . . . N—B3 Variation

WHITE	BLACK		WHITE	BLACK
1 P—K4	P—K4		3 B—B4	B—B4
2 N—KB3	N—QB3		4 P—B3	N—B3

The classic counterattacking move. Black intends to give up the center with his next move.

| 5 P—Q4 | PxP | | 6 PxP | . . . . |

Note that although 6 P—K5 looks impressive, Black has a perfect answer in 6 . . . P—Q4!

| 6 . . . . | B—N5ch |

29

(Position after 6 . . . B—N5ch)

The simple and safe course is now 7 B—Q2, BxBch; 8 QNxB, P—Q4!; 9 PxP, KNxP; 10 Q—N3, QN—K2; 11 Castles, Castles with equality.

The alternative 6 . . . B—N3? leaves Black with a miserable game after 7 P—K5, N—KN1; 8 P—Q5 etc.

7 N—B3?! NxKP!?

Another way is 7 . . . P—Q4! and if 8 PxP, KNxP; 9 Castles, B—K3!; 10 B—KN5, B—K2; 11 BxN, QBxB; 12 NxB, QxN; 13 BxB, NxB; 14 R—K1, P—KB3!; 15 Q—K2, Q—Q2; 16 QR—B1, K—B2! and Black is safe after 17 . . . KR—K1 and 18 . . . K—N1.

Note that White's last move is a wild attempt to create dangerous complications at the cost of a Pawn or even more material.

8 Castles . . . .

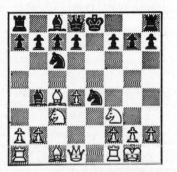

30

(Position after 8 Castles)

Black must proceed with great care.

Now 8 . . . NxN can lead to a lot of trouble for Black after 9 PxN, P—Q4; 10 PxB, PxB; 11 R—K1ch, N—K2 (if 11 . . . B—K3?; 12 P—Q5 wins a piece); 12 Q—K2, B—K3; 13 B—N5, Q—Q4; 14 BxN, KxB; 15 Q—B2!, P—KB3; 16 N—N5!, PxN (if 16 . . . QxN; 17 Q—K4 with a winning attack); 17 R—K5, QxQP; 18 QR—K1 and White wins back his piece with advantage.

Another dangerous line for Black is 8 . . . NxN; 9 PxN, BxP?; 10 B—R3!! and wins. Thus, after 10 . . . BxR??; 11 R—K1ch Black can resign.

And if 10 . . . P—Q4; 11 B—N5!, BxR; 12 R—K1ch, B—K3; 13 Q—R4! and Black is lost.

Or take this possibility: 10 . . . P—Q3; 11 R—B1, B—R4; 12 Q—R4, P—QR3; 13 B—Q5, B—N3; 14 RxN!, B—Q2; 15 R—K1ch, K—B1; 16 RxQP!! and wins.

| 8 . . . . | BxN! | 9 P—Q5 | . . . . |

31

(Position after 9 P—Q5)

This position is full of bewildering possibilities. Black's safest is 9 . . . N—K4!

| 9 . . . | N—K4! | 10 PxB | NxB |
| | 11 Q—Q4 | . . . . | |

A famous trap here is 11 . . . N/B5—Q3?; 12 QxNP, Q—B3; 13 QxQ, NxQ; 14 R—K1ch. If now 14 . . . K—Q1??; 15 B—N5! wins. If 14 . . . K—B1??; 15 B—R6ch, K—N1; 16 R—K5! and Black is lost, for example 16 . . . N/Q3—K5; 17 N—Q2, NxN; 18 R—KN5 mate or 17 . . . P—Q3; 18 NxN, PxR; 19 NxN mate.

Finally, if 14 . . . N/B3—K5; 15 N—Q2, P—B4; 16 P—B3 with a winning game for White.

| 11 . . . . | P—KB4 | 12 QxN/B4 | . . . . |

Not 12 QxNP?, Q—B3 and White has no compensation for the lost piece.

12 ....   P—Q3

Black has the advantage: his position is safe and he is a Pawn to the good.

(b) 4 . . . Q—K2 Variation

WHITE	BLACK		WHITE	BLACK
1 P—K4	P—K4		3 B—B4	B—B4
2 N—KB3	N—QB3		4 P—B3	Q—K2
	5 P—Q4	B—N3		

32

(Position after 5 . . . B—N3)

Black avoids exchanging Pawns in order to hold the center. The result is a very cramped game for him.

6 Castles	N—B3		7 R—K1	P—Q3
	8 P—KR3!	....		

Preventing the pin . . . B—N5. Thus White strengthens his Pawn center and deprives Black's Queen Bishop of its best square.

8	Castles		10 B—Q3!	P—B3
9 N—R3!	N—Q1		11 N—B4	B—B2

White has distinctly the better game because of his greater freedom. He can play 12 P—QN3! threatening 13 B—R3 with annoying possibilities.

(c) 4 P—Q3 Variation

WHITE	BLACK	WHITE	BLACK
1 P—K4	P—K4	3 B—B4	B—B4
2 N—KB3	N—QB3	4 P—Q3	....

This leads to a slow game which gives Black very little trouble.

4	N—B3	5 N—B3	P—Q3
	6 B—K3	....	

After 6 B—KN5, P—KR3 (6 . . . N—QR4 is also playable); 7 BxN, QxB; 8 N—Q5, Q—Q1; 9 P—B3, P—R3!; 10 P—Q4, PxP; 11 PxP, B—R2 Black's game is slightly preferable because of his two Bishops.

6	B—N3

Better than 6 . . . BxB; 7 PxB, which gives White an open King Bishop file.

7 Q—Q2	B—K3	8 B—N3	....

White is confronted with the same problem that Black encountered at move 6. That is to say, White is unwilling to play BxB, for that would open the King Bishop file for Black. However, now that White has retreated B—N3, Black in turn has to meet the same problem. If Black now plays 8 . . . BxB, White replies 9 RPxB, acquiring an open Queen Rook file.

This reasoning about the desirability or undesirability of exchanging the Bishops is an important feature of the variation. Obtaining an open file is often the imperceptible beginning of a strong initiative.

33
(Position after 8 B—N3)

This is a good variation for inexperienced players, as the position offers little scope for complications.

Even game; the symmetrical position of the Bishops and Pawns offers little to either side.

EVANS GAMBIT

The Evans is a brilliant offshoot of the Giuoco Piano, wherein White sacrifices a Pawn in order to obtain open lines and gain time to form a strong Pawn center. The attack can become extremely vehement and calls for really resourceful play on the defender's part.

(a) Evans Gambit Accepted

WHITE	BLACK		WHITE	BLACK
1 P—K4	P—K4		3 B—B4	B—B4
2 N—KB3	N—QB3		4 P—QN4	....

34

(Position after 4 P—QN4)

White offers a Pawn sacrifice which may involve many pitfalls, prepared variations, and tricky analysis. Black does well to choose a simple defense.

4	BxNP	5 P—B3	B—K2!

The old defense 5 . . . B—B4; 6 P—Q4, PxP; 7 PxP, B—N3; 8 Castles, P—Q3 leaves White with a strong lead in development after 9 N—B3.

6 P—Q4	N—QR4!

Guarding against 7 Q—N3.

7 B—Q3	....

Or 7 NxP, NxB; 8 NxN, P—Q4; 9 PxP, QxP with a pleasant game for Black.

| 7 .... | PxP | 8 PxP | P—Q4 |

If now 9 PxP, N—KB3; 10 Q—R4ch, P—B3 and Black's game is very comfortable.

| 9 N—B3 | PxP | 11 NxNch | BxN |
| 10 NxP | N—KB3 | 12 Q—R4ch | N—B3 |

Black has an easy game after 13 B—R3, B—K2; 14 B—N5, Castles! returning the gambit Pawn. Note Black's emphasis on quick development—even at the cost of returning the gambit Pawn.

(b) Evans Gambit Declined

WHITE	BLACK	WHITE	BLACK
1 P—K4	P—K4	3 B—B4	B—B4
2 N—KB3	N—QB3	4 P—QN4	B—N3!
	5 P—QR4	....	

35

(Position after 5 P—QR4)

By declining the gambit Black gets a perfectly safe and satisfactory position. Thus he avoids all the complications of the gambit accepted.

5	P—QR3	9 BxR	N—Q5!
6 B—N2	P—Q3	10 NxN	PxN
7 P—N5	PxP	11 P—QB3	N—B3
8 PxP	RxR	12 Castles	Castles

Even game, with this possibility: 13 P—Q3, P—B3!; 14 NPxP, NPxP; 15 PxP, P—Q4!; 16 PxP, NxP and White's extra Pawn is worthless.

TWO KNIGHTS' DEFENSE

This is a line of play frequently selected by those who wish to evade the Giuoco Piano or Evans Gambit. This defense calls for enterprising play, as many variations necessitate a Pawn sacrifice on Black's part.

(a) 4 N—N5 Variation

WHITE	BLACK		WHITE	BLACK
1 P—K4	P—K4		3 B—B4	N—B3
2 N—KB3	N—QB3		4 N—N5	P—Q4
	5 PxP		....	

36

(Position after 5 PxP)

Black's best is 5 ... NxP!, for if 6 NxBP?! (the Fried Liver Attack), KxN; 7 Q—B3ch, K—K3; 8 N—B3, QN—N5!; 9 Q—K4, P—B3; 10 P—Q4, K—Q2! and Black is safe.

5	N—QR4	6 B—N5ch	....

After 6 P—Q3, P—KR3; 7 N—KB3, P—K5 Black has the initiative in return for his sacrificed Pawn; for example 8 Q—K2, NxB; 9 PxN, B—QB4; 10 KN—Q2, Castles; 11 N—N3, B—KN5! etc.

6	P—B3	7 PxP	PxP
	8 B—K2	....	

On 8 Q—B3 Black can try the venturesome 8 ... PxB!; 9 QxR, Q—Q2! with a notable lead in development against White's disorganized forces.

8	P—KR3		12 Castles!	BxN
9 N—KB3	P—K5		13 PxB	Q—Q5ch
10 N—K5	B—Q3		14 K—R1	QxKP
11 P—KB4!	Castles		15 P—Q4!	....

37

(Position after 15 P—Q4!)

White has benefited considerably by returning the Pawn at move 12.

White has the better game whether Black retreats his Queen or captures his Queen Pawn in passing. White's positional advantages are well-defined: he has an open King Bishop file, two aggressive Bishops, the Queen-side majority of Pawns. Black's Queen-side Pawns are split and his Queen Knight is sadly out of play.

(b) 4 P—Q4 Variation

WHITE	BLACK		WHITE	BLACK
1 P—K4	P—K4		3 B—B4	N—B3
2 N—KB3	N—QB3		4 P—Q4	PxP
	5 Castles		NxP	

The alternative 5 . . . B—B4; 6 P—K5, P—Q4 may lead to the Max Lange Attack (page 46).

6 R—K1	P—Q4		7 BxP	QxB
	8 N—B3		....	

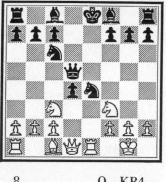

38

(Position after 8 N—B3)

White makes use of a piquant double pin to win back the sacrificed material.

8	Q—KR4	10 B—N5	B—QN5
9 NxN	B—K3	11 NxP	....

White has regained his Pawn with an even game. The continuation might be: 11 . . . QxQ; 12 KRxQ, NxN; 13 RxN, B—K2.

(c) Max Lange Attack

WHITE	BLACK	WHITE	BLACK
1 P—K4	P—K4	5 Castles	B—B4
2 N—KB3	N—QB3	6 P—K5	P—Q4!
3 B—B4	N—B3	7 PxN	PxB
4 P—Q4	PxP	8 R—K1ch	....

White should play for equality with 8 PxP, KR—N1; 9 B—N5 etc.

8	B—K3	9 N—N5	....

39

(Position after 9 N—N5)

White's threat is 10 NxB, PxN; 11 Q—R5ch winning the Bishop.

9	Q—Q4	10 N—QB3!	Q—B4
11 QN—K4	....		

If now 11 . . . B—KB1; 12 NxBP!, KxN; 13 N—N5ch and White regains the piece with a winning attack.

11	Castles QR!	13 P—KN4	Q—K4
12 N/N5xB	PxN	14 PxP	KR—N1

In this wide-open position Black has the initiative, for example 15 B—R6, B—N5!; 16 R—K2, P—Q6! etc.

FOUR KNIGHTS' GAME
(including Three Knights' Game)

This stolid line of play is generally good for a draw, but unpromising if White wants to play for a win. Black has many equalizing methods, and numerous possibilities of simplifying exchanges.

(a) 6 . . . BxN Variation

WHITE	BLACK		WHITE	BLACK
1 P—K4	P—K4		4 B—N5	B—N5
2 N—KB3	N—QB3		5 Castles	Castles
3 N—B3	N—B3		6 P—Q3	. . . .

A lifeless, drawish alternative is 6 BxN, NPxB; 7 NxP, R—K1; 8 N—Q3, BxN; 9 QPxB, NxP etc.

6	BxN	7 PxB	P—Q3
8 B—N5	Q—K2		

After 8 . . . N—K2?; 9 BxN, PxB; 10 N—R4, P—B3; 11 B—B4, P—Q4; 12 B—N3, N—N3; 13 NxN, RPxN; 14 P—KB4! White has a decided initiative.

9 R—K1	N—Q1

40
(Position after 9 . . . N—Q1)

Black rearranges his pieces to get more maneuvering freedom.

10 P—Q4   N—K3   11 B—QB1   P—B4!

Black does not fear 12 PxP, PxP; 13 NxP?? for then 13
. . . N—B2! wins a piece.

            12 P—N3   Q—B2

*Black has a slight advantage because of his superior Pawn
position. A plausible possibility is 13 Q—K2, P—QR3; 14
B—Q3, P—QN4; 15 P—Q5, P—B5!; 16 PxN, BxP! and
Black regains the piece favorably.*

(b) 6 . . . P—Q3 Variation

	WHITE	BLACK
1	P—K4	P—K4
2	N—KB3	N—QB3
3	N—B3	N—B3

	WHITE	BLACK
4	B—N5	B—N5
5	Castles	Castles
6	P—Q3	P—Q3

41

(Position after 6 . . . P—Q3)

*Black intends to hold on to the two
Bishops. If now 7 N—K2 Black replies 7 . . . N—K2 with a symmetrical, drawish position.*

            7 B—N5   N—K2

And not 7 . . . B—N5 because of 8 N—Q5 intensifying
the pin on Black's King Knight.

8 BxN	PxB
9 N—KR4	N—N3
10 NxN	RPxN

11 P—B4	B—B4ch
12 K—R1	K—N2
13 P—B5	....

After 13 ... P—B3; 14 B—B4, P—Q4! Black's Bishop-pair and compact Pawn center promise well for him despite the somewhat barricaded character of the position.

(c) 4 ... N—Q5 Variation

WHITE	BLACK
1 P—K4	P—K4
2 N—KB3	N—QB3
	5 NxP

WHITE	BLACK
3 N—B3	N—B3
4 B—N5	N—Q5
Q—K2	

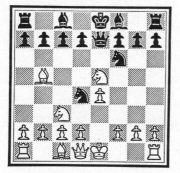

42

(Position after 5 ... Q—K2)

Black has violated the rules of good development, but how is he to be punished? If 6 N—B3, NxB; 7 NxN, QxPch; 8 Q—K2, QxQch; 9 KxQ, N—Q4; 10 P—B4, P—QR3! and White has nothing.

6 P—B4!	NxB
7 NxN	P—Q3
8 N—KB3	QxPch

9 K—B2	N—N5ch
10 K—N1!	K—Q1
11 P—Q3	Q—B3

After 12 QN—Q4, Q—N3; 13 P—KR3, N—B3; 14 K—R2 White has the better game. Black's King is insecure, his development disorganized.

(d) Three Knights' Game

WHITE	BLACK		WHITE	BLACK
1 P—K4	P—K4		2 N—KB3	N—QB3
	3 N—B3		B—N5	

43

(Position after 3 . . . B N5)

Black's last move is the key to this opening. If instead 3 . . . N—B3 we have the Four Knights' Game.

4 N—Q5	N—B3		5 NxB	NxN

If now 6 P—Q4, P—Q4! — or 6 B—B4, P—Q4!; 7 PxP, P K5! with equality in either event.

6 NxP	Q—K2		9 NxN	QPxN
7 P—Q4	NxKP		10 B—K2	Castles
8 P—QB3	N—QB3		11 Castles	B K3

Even game. Neither side can accomplish much in this colorless position.

In the whole realm of the King Pawn openings, this is White's most serious attempt to seize the initiative. There are many lines of play in which White maintains a lasting pressure on Black's position. Undoubtedly Black's best defense is some form of the "Strong-point" Variation, for this gives him his best chance of freedom.

(a) Morphy Defense with 5 . . . B—K2

WHITE	BLACK		WHITE	BLACK
1 P—K4	P—K4		2 N—KB3	N—QB3
3 B—N5	. . . .			

This move exercises unmistakable pressure on Black's game. Sooner or later White will be threatening to win a Pawn by BxN followed by NxP.

44
(Position after 3 B—N5)

Black can play 3 . . . P—QR3 for if 4 BxN, QPxB; 5 NxP, Black recovers his Pawn with 5 . . . Q—N4 or . . . Q—Q5.

3 . . . .   P—QR3

This (known as the Morphy Defense) is Black's best. By driving off White's King Bishop with an eventual . . . P—QN4, Black rids himself of White's potential threat to win the King Pawn and gives his forces more playing room.

A possibility here for White is the Exchange Variation,

which does not have much sting: 4 BxN, QPxB. This may continue 5 P—Q4, PxP; 6 QxP, QxQ; 7 NxQ, B—Q2; 8 B—K3, Castles; 9 N—Q2, N—K2; 10 Castles QR, R—K1; 11 KR—K1, N—N3. Black's Bishops give him an excellent game.

4 B—R4   N—B3

A good developing move which gains time by attacking White's King Pawn.

5 Castles   ....

Momentarily White can leave his King Pawn in the lurch, as he has threats on Black's King Pawn himself.

5 ....   B—K2

Black can also play 5 . . . NxP, as in Variation *(c)*.

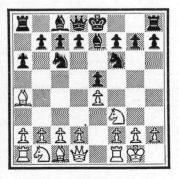

45

(Position after 5 . . . B—K2)

White can now choose between defending his King Pawn and advancing in the center by P—Q4.

If White advances 6 P—Q4, Black's best reply is 6 . . . PxP. In that event White should not pause for 7 R—K1, as he may fall into the Noah's Ark Trap: 7 . . . P—QN4; 8 B—N3, P—Q3; 9 NxP??, NxN; 10 QxN, P—B4 followed by . . . P—B5 winning White's King Bishop!

In reply to 6 . . . PxP White's best course is 7 P—K5. Then, after 7 . . . N—K5; 8 NxP, NxN (not 8 . . . NxKP??; 9 R—K1); 9 QxN, N—B4 the position is fairly level: White gets a lead in development, while Black has the two Bishops.

Coming back to the position of Diagram 45, White can also stop to defend his King Pawn with 6 Q—K2. Then if 6 . . . Castles? there follows 7 BxN, QPxB; 8 NxP, Q—Q5; 9 N—KB3, QxKP; 10 QxQ, NxQ; 11 R—K1 and White wins a piece.

Consequently, after 6 Q—K2 Black plays 6 . . . P—Q3, although after 7 P—B3, Castles; 8 P—Q4 his game is somewhat constricted.

6 R—K1   . . . .

This is the usual move. Now that White has protected his own King Pawn, he threatens to win a Pawn by 7 BxN and 8 NxP.

6 . . . .   P—QN4

Driving off the Bishop in order to safeguard his King Pawn.

7 B—N3   P—Q3

The safe and sane course, which avoids the premature counterattack 7 . . . Castles; 8 P—B3, P—Q4?!

In that event there may follow 9 PxP, NxP; 10 NxP, NxN; 11 RxN, P—QB3; 12 P—Q4!, B—Q3; 13 R—K1, Q—R5; 14 P—N3, Q—R6; 15 R—K4!

Although Black still has some attacking prospects, White has a satisfactory defense. His extra Pawn should tell in his favor.

8 P—B3   Castles   9 P—KR3!   . . . .

More precise than the immediate 9 P—Q4, which would allow the pin 9 . . . B—N5. By advancing his King Rook Pawn, White deprives Black's Queen Bishop of his best square.

| 9 .... | N—QR4! | 10 B—B2 | P—B4 |
| | 11 P—Q4 | Q—B2 | |

46

(Position after 11 . . . Q—B2)

Black has established a "strong point" at King 4. By advancing his Queenside Pawns (beginning with 3 . . . P—QR3) he has established ample maneuvering space for his forces.

| | 12 QN—Q2 | N—B3 |

A plausible alternative is 12 . . . BPxP; 13 PxP, N—B3; 14 P—Q5, N—QN5; 15 B—N1, P—QR4; 16 P—R3, N—R3. Black's Queen Knight will come to Queen Bishop 4, but White's game is slightly freer.

| 13 P—Q5 | N—Q1 | 14 P—QR4! | R—N1 |

But not 14 . . . P—N5, which allows White to post his Queen Knight magnificently at Bishop 4.

| 15 P—B4! | P—N5 | 17 P—KN4 | P—N3 |
| 16 N—B1 | N—K1 | 18 B—R6 | N—KN2 |

The position is approximately even. White has more maneuvering space, but Black's game is very compact and hard to get at.

(b) Morphy Defense with 4 . . . P—Q3

	WHITE	BLACK		WHITE	BLACK
1	P—K4	P—K4	3	B—N5	P—QR3
2	N—KB3	N—QB3	4	B—R4	P—Q3

47

(Position after 4 . . . P—Q3)

Black has delayed playing out his King Knight as he has in mind variations in which this piece may play to King 2 or King Rook 3; he may also want to advance his King Bishop Pawn.

If now 5 BxNch, PxB; 6 P—Q4 Black holds the center with 6 . . . P—B3! and after 7 B—K3, N—K2; 8 N—B3, N—N3; 9 Q—Q2, B—K2 his position is satisfactory.

Another possibility is 5 P—Q4, P—QN4; 6 B—N3, NxP; 7 NxN, PxN. Now 8 B—Q5 is satisfactory for White, whereas 8 QxP??, P—QB4; 9 Q—Q5, B—K3; 10 Q—B6ch, B—Q2; 11 Q—Q5, P—B5 gives us another version of the Noah's Ark Trap.

5 P—B3   B—Q2

Here 5 . . . P—B4 is premature: 6 PxP, BxP; 7 P—Q4!, P—K5; 8 N—N5, P—Q4; 9 P—B3! forcing line-opening which is distinctly in White's favor.

	WHITE	BLACK		WHITE	BLACK
6	P—Q4	P—KN3	10	P—KR3	N—B2
7	B—KN5	P—B3	11	QN—Q2	Castles
8	B—K3	N—R3!	12	PxP	QPxP
9	Castles	B—N2	13	B—B5	R—K1

The position is approximately even. White's apparent pressure is neutralized by Black's solid position.

(c) Morphy Defense with 5 . . . NxP

WHITE	BLACK		WHITE	BLACK
1 P—K4	P—K4		4 B—R4	N—B3
2 N—KB3	N—QB3		5 Castles	NxP
3 B—N5	P—QR3		6 P—Q4!	....

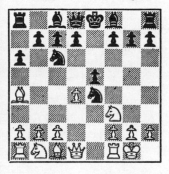

48

(Position after 6 P—Q4!)

Winning a second Pawn leads to trouble for Black, for example: 6 . . . PxP; 7 R—K1, P—Q4; 8 B—KN5!, Q—Q3; 9 P—B4!, PxP e.p.; 10 NxP, B—K3; 11 NxN, PxN; 12 N—Q4, P—N4; 13 RxP!, PxB; 14 QxP, Q—Q4; 15 R—K5!! and wins.

6	P—QN4		8 PxP	B—K3
7 B—N3	P—Q4		9 P—B3	....

An interesting possibility is 9 Q—K2, for example 9 . . . N—B4; 10 R—Q1, NxB; 11 RPxN, Q—B1; 12 P—B4!, QPxP; 13 PxP, BxP; 14 Q—K4 and White has a winning attack.

49

(Position after 9 P—B3)

Here 9 . . . B—QB4 gives Black an aggressive development but leaves him with a vulnerable Pawn position —for example 10 Q—Q3, Castles; 11 B—K3, BxB; 12 QxB, N—K2; 13 B—B2, P—KB4; 14 PxP e.p., RxP; 15 N—Q4!

9	B—K2		10 P—QR4!	....

Now White gets a strong initiative.

10	P—N5	12 P—KB4	B—N5
11 N—Q4!	NxKP	13 Q—B2	P—QB4

Not 13 . . . N—N3; 14 PxP, BxP?; 15 N—B6.

14 PxN	PxN	15 PxQP	Castles

White has a clear advantage because of his greater mobility, attacking chances, prospects of creating weaknesses in Black's King-side.

(d) Berlin Defense

WHITE	BLACK	WHITE	BLACK
1 P—K4	P—K4	2 N—KB3	N—QB3
3 B—N5	N—B3		

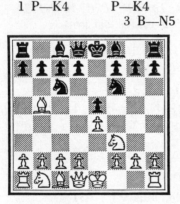

50

(Position after 3 . . . N—B3)

The drawback of this once-popular defense is that it leads to a weak Pawn position for Black.

4 Castles	NxP	5 P—Q4	B—K2

Note that 5 . . . PxP?? will not do because of 6 R—K1.

6 Q—K2	N—Q3	10 N—Q4	B—B4
7 BxN	NPxB	11 R—Q1	BxN
8 PxP	N—N2	12 RxB	P—Q4
9 N—B3	Castles	13 PxP.e.p.	PxP

The position is decidedly in White's favor. Black's game

is very difficult because of his weak Pawns and the bad position of his Knight.

(e) Steinitz Defense

WHITE	BLACK		WHITE	BLACK
1 P—K4	P—K4		2 N—KB3	N—QB3
	3 B—N5	P—Q3		

This defense gives Black a cramped game.

4 P—Q4!	B—Q2		5 N—B3	N—B3

If instead 5 . . . PxP; 6 NxP, N—B3; 7 BxN!, PxB; 8 Q—B3! and White has the better of it, for example 8 . . . B—K2; 9 P—K5!, PxP; 10 NxP etc.

	6 Castles	B—K2

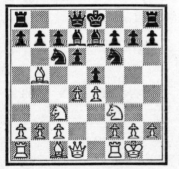

51

(Position after 6 . . . B—K2)

A likely continuation is 7 B—N5!, PxP; 8 NxP, Castles; 9 BxQN, PxB; 10 Q—Q3, N—N5; 11 BxB, QxB; 12 P—B4!, P—KB4; 13 QR—K1!

White has the better game. His aggressive development gives him much greater freedom of action.

(f) Classical Defense

WHITE	BLACK		WHITE	BLACK
1 P—K4	P—K4		2 N—KB3	N—QB3
	3 B—N5	B—B4		

52
(Position after 3 ... B—B4)

The drawback to this defense is that Black's King Bishop becomes a target for attack.

4 Castles	KN—K2		9 R—K1ch	B—K3
5 P—B3	B—N3		10 BxNch!	PxB
6 P—Q4	PxP		11 Q—R4	Q—Q3
7 PxP	P—Q4		12 B—N5	Castles
8 PxP	KNxP		13 N—B3	....

Thanks to Black's shattered Pawn position, White has a strategically won game.

(g) Bird's Defense

WHITE	BLACK		WHITE	BLACK
1 P—K4	P—K4		2 N—KB3	N—QB3
	3 B—N5	N—Q5		

53
(Position after 3 ... N—Q5)

This defense lacks punch. The offered exchange wastes time and allows White to get a clear initiative on the King-side.

4 NxN	PxN	9 N—B3	P—QB3
5 Castles	P—KN3	10 B—QR4	P—Q3
6 P—Q3	B—N2	11 B—K3!	B—N2
7 P—QB3!	N—K2	12 Q—B3	Castles
8 PxP	BxP	13 B—N3	K—R1
	14 Q—N3	....	

White is clearly forcing the pace, while Black has a difficult defensive game.

(h) Schliemann's Defense

WHITE	BLACK	WHITE	BLACK
1 P—K4	P—K4	2 N—KB3	N—QB3
	3 B—N5	P—B4	

54

(Position after 3 . . . P—B4)

Black's counterattack is risky and invites a brisk reaction by White.

4 N—B3!	PxP	8 BxPch	B—Q2
5 QNxP	P—Q4	9 Q—R5ch	K—K2
6 NxP!	PxN	10 Q—K5ch	B—K3
7 NxN	PxN	11 BxR	QxB

White is ahead in material and Black's King is exposed to attack.

FRENCH DEFENSE

From this point on, we no longer consider openings in which Black answers 1 P—K4 with 1 . . . P—K4. Instead, he tries to fight for control of the center in a different way.

In this opening, for example, he answers 1 P—K4 with 1 . . . P—K3, and then, after 2 P—Q4, he continues 2 . . . P—Q4. This is a defense with many solid defensive virtues, with the notable drawback that in many lines Black's Queen Bishop has little scope.

This explains why the simplifying course 3 PxP, PxP is rarely seen in modern play. The Pawn position is symmetrical and drawish, and Black's Queen Bishop has been liberated. Most variations in which White gets the initiative involve the move P—K5. This keeps Black's Queen Bishop tied up and also offers prospects of King-side attack.

(a) McCutcheon Variation

WHITE	BLACK		WHITE	BLACK
1 P—K4	P—K3		3 N—QB3	N—KB3
2 P—Q4	P—Q4		4 B—KN5	B—N5

Black fights vigorously for control of the center. If now 5 PxP, QxP; 6 BxN, BxNch; 7 PxB, PxB; 8 N—KB3, N—Q2; 9 P—N3, P—N3; 10 B—N2 and Black can play 10 . . . B—R3!, for if 11 N—R4, Q—QR4!; 12 BxR, QxBPch and wins.

5 P—K5	P—KR3

Forced. If now 6 PxN, PxB; 7 PxP, R—N1 regaining the Pawn with equality.

6 B—Q2	BxN		7 PxB	N—K5
			8 Q—N4	P—KN3

55

(Position after 8 . . . P—KN3)

Now White tries a speculative sacrifice to preserve his valuable Queen Bishop, for if 9 B—Q3, NxB; 10 KxN, P—QB4 with a good game for Black.

9 B—B1!?	NxQBP	11 PxP	Q—B2
10 B—Q3	P—QB4	12 B—K3	N—Q2

With 13 Q—Q4! White maintains the initiative, and his two powerful Bishops assure him substantial attacking chances.

(b) 4 . . . B—K2 Variation

WHITE	BLACK	WHITE	BLACK
1 P—K4	P—K3	3 N—QB3	N—KB3
2 P—Q4	P—Q4	4 B—KN5	B—K2

Another way of fighting for the center. White can hit back with 5 BxN, BxB; 6 P—K5, but after 6 . . . B—K2; 7 Q—N4, Castles; 8 Castles, P—QB4! Black has good counterplay. For example: 9 PxP, N—B3; 10 P—B4, P—B4; 11 Q—R3, Q—R4!; 12 KN—K2, BxP; 13 P—KN4, P—Q5; 14 N—QN1, N—QN5 and Black has the initiative.

5 P—K5	KN—Q2	7 Q—Q2	Castles
6 BxB	QxB	8 P—B4	P—QB4
	9 N—B3	N—QB3	

56

(Position after 9 . . . N—QB3)

Black has attacked White's Pawn center with . . . P—QB4 and intends to intensify the attack with . . . P—B3.

If now 10 P—KN3, P—B3; 11 KPxP, NPxP! as in the main line, with a promising game for Black.

10	Castles	P—B3		12	P—KN3	PxP
11	KPxP	NPxP!		13	KNxP	N—N3

Even game. White may have the better development, but Black has open lines and a powerful Pawn mass in the center.

(c) Alekhine's Attack

	WHITE	BLACK			WHITE	BLACK
1	P—K4	P—K3		4	B—KN5	B—K2
2	P—Q4	P—Q4		5	P—K5	KN—Q2
3	N—QB3	N—KB3		6	P—KR4!	....

57

(Position after 6 P—KR4!)

Black cannot very well accept White's enterprising Pawn offer. After 6 . . . BxB; 7 PxB, QxP; 8 N—R3, Q—K2; 9 N—B4, N—B1; 10 Q—N4 White has a murderous lead in development.

If now 6 . . . P—KB3; 7 Q—R5ch!, P—KN3; 8 PxP!, PxQ; 9 PxB winning back the Queen with a very superior endgame for White; or 8 . . . NxP; 9 Q—K2! with strong pressure on Black's backward King Pawn.

| 6 .... | P—QB4! | 7 BxB | KxB! |

After 7 . . . QxB; 8 N—N5! Black has a difficult game.

| 8 Q—N4 | K—B1 | 10 QxQP | Q—N3! |
| 9 N—B3 | PxP! | 11 QxQ | PxQ |

Black has satisfactorily undermined White's center.

| 12 Castles | N—QB3 | 13 R—K1 | P—Q5! |

Black has an excellent game, for after the attacked Knight moves he can play . . . RxP.

(d) 4 . . . PxP Variation

WHITE	BLACK	WHITE	BLACK
1 P—K4	P—K3	2 P—Q4	P—Q4
	3 N—QB3	N—KB3	

58

(Position after 3 . . . N—KB3)

If White ends the tension in the center with 4 P—-K5, there follows 4 . . . KN—Q2; 5 P—B4 and now Black counters with 5 . . . P—QB4! liquidating White's valuable Queen Pawn.

4 B—KN5	PxP

This colorless continuation leaves White with a more aggressive position.

5 NxP	B—K2	6 BxN	BxB

Likewise after 6 . . . PxB White has the more promising development: 7 N—KB3, P—N3; 8 B—B4!, B—N2; 9 Q—K2, P—B3; 10 Castles QR, Q—B2; 11 K—N1, N—Q2; 12 B—R6!, Castles QR; 13 BxBch, KxB; 14 P—B4! Black's Pawn position is weakened and he is exposed to attack.

7 N—KB3	N—Q2	8 P—B3!	Q—K2

Or 8 . . . Castles; 9 Q—B2, P—K4; 10 Castles!, PxP; 11 NxP, BxN; 12 RxB, Q—K2; 13 P—KB4, N—B4; 14 NxN, QxN; 15 B—Q3 when White has a splendid development and good attacking chances.

9 Q—B2	P—B4	12 BxBch	NxB
10 PxP	NxP	13 Castles QR	Castles QR
11 B—N5ch	B—Q2	14 Q—R4	K—N1

White's game is more comfortable and he has an advantage for the endgame in his Queen-side majority of Pawns.

(e)   3 . . . B—N5 Variation

WHITE	BLACK	WHITE	BLACK
1 P—K4	P—K3	2 P—Q4	P—Q4
	3 N—QB3	B—N5	

59
(Position after 3 . . . B—N5)

By pinning White's Knight Black counterattacks and thus maintains the fight for control of the center. 4 PxP would be a colorless reply as 4 . . . PxP frees Black's Queen Bishop.

White can ignore Black's threat, but the results are not particularly attractive, for example 4 P—QR3, BxNch; 5 PxB, PxP; 6 Q—N4, N—KB3; 7 QxNP, R—N1; 8 Q—R6, P—B4—or 4 Q—N4, N—KB3; 5 QxNP, R—N1; 6 Q—R6, P—B4. In either case Black has strong counterplay.

| 4 P—K5 | P—QB4 | 5 P—QR3! | .... |

The best reply to Black's logical counterattack in the center.

| 5 .... | BxNch | 6 PxB | .... |

Whereas Black's remaining Bishop has very little scope, White's Bishops are very powerful—as in the variation 6 . . . N—K2; 7 Q—N4, N—B4; 8 B—Q3, P—KR4; 9 Q—R3, PxP; 10 PxP, Q—R5; 11 QxQ, NxQ; 12 P—N3 etc.

| 6 .... | Q—B2 | 7 N—B3 | .... |

After Black's last move, he can answer 7 Q—N4 with 7 . . . P—B4.

| 7 .... | N—K2 | 8 P—KR4! | B—Q2 |

Striving for counterplay. If instead 8 . . . P—QN3; 9 P—R5!, P—KR3; 10 P—R4!, B—R3; 11 B—N5ch!, BxB; 12 PxB and White has the initiative on both wings.

$$9 \text{ P—R5} \qquad \text{P—KR3}$$

White was threatening 10 P—R6 practically forcing . . . P—KN3 and leaving Black dangerously weak on the black squares.

10 P—N4!	B—R5		12 P—N5	QR—B1
11 B—Q3	N—Q2		13 R—QR2!	....

White has a strong initiative on the King-side, where he will be able to open a file before or after R—N1. Black has pressure on White's Pawn at Queen Bishop 2, but White has adequate defense. White's greater command of the Board, supported by the potential power of his Bishops, gives him the better game.

(*f*) 3 N—Q2 Variation

WHITE	BLACK		WHITE	BLACK
1 P—K4	P—K3		2 P—Q4	P—Q4
	3 N—Q2		....	

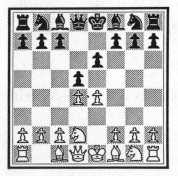

60
(Position after 3 N—Q2)

White's extraordinary third move is playable despite the fact that it blocks his Queen Bishop. The point of this development is that it avoids 3 . . . B—N5, as seen in Variation (e).

3 ....   P—QB4

The classic freeing move. The alternatives give Black a
cramped game, for example 3 . . . N—KB3; 4 P—K5, KN—
Q2; 5 B—Q3, P—QB4; 6 P—QB3, N—QB3; 7 N—K2,
PxP; 8 PxP etc. Or 3 . . . N—QB3; 4 KN—B3!, N—B3;
5 P—K5, N—Q2; 6 N—N3, P—B3; 7 PxP!, KNxP; 8 B—
QN5 etc.

4 KN—B3   P—QR3!

This gives Black a much more comfortable game than 4
. . . N—QB3, for example 5 KPxP, KPxP; 6 B—N5!, B—
Q3; 7 Castles, N—K2; 8 PxP!, BxBP; 9 N—N3, B—N3;
10 B—K3!, BxB; 11 BxNch!, PxB; 12 PxB and White has
strong pressure on the black squares.

5 KPxP   KPxP   6 PxP   BxP

Black has an isolated Queen Pawn, but he can develop his
pieces rapidly and the diagonal of his Queen Bishop has
been opened.

7 N—N3	B—R2!	10 B—K2	Q—Q3
8 B—KN5	N—KB3	11 Castles	N—B3!
9 QN—Q4	Castles	12 B—K3	B—N1!

*Black has real attacking chances and a fine initiative. His
admirable development outweighs the disadvantage of the
isolated Queen Pawn.*

(g) 3 P—K5 Variation

WHITE	BLACK		WHITE	BLACK
1 P—K4	P—K3		2 P—Q4	P—Q4
3 P—K5!?	P—QB4!			

This is an extremely trying variation for both players. By advancing his Pawn to King 5, White creates a wedge in the King-side which among other things prevents Black's Knight from reaching its best square at Black's King Bishop 3. In general, White's intention when he advances the King Pawn is to leave Black with a permanently constricted position.

Naturally Black is not going to resign himself to being smothered to death. He intends to fight back, and the method he chooses is to try to undermine White's advanced King Pawn by removing its support (White's Queen Pawn).

61
(Position after 3 . . . P—QB4!)

By playing . . . P—QB4 — always the logical counterattack to P—K5 — Black strives for counterplay on the Queen-side and in the center in order to neutralize White's constricting pressure on the King-side.

4 P—QB3	N—QB3		5 N—KB3	Q—N3

Superficially 6 B—Q3 looks like a good reply, for if 6 . . . PxP; 7 PxP, NxQP???; 8 NxN, QxN; 9 B—QN5ch winning the Queen. But Black plays 6 . . . PxP; 7 PxP, B—Q2! leaving White nothing better than 8 B—K2.

| 6 B—K2 | PxP | 8 P—QN3 | N—B4 |
| 7 PxP | KN—K2 | 9 B—N2 | B—N5ch |

Black's pressure on the Queen Pawn is so strong that White cannot interpose to this check.

| 10 K—B1 | Castles | 11 P—N4 | N—R3 |

After 12 R—N1 Black plays 12 . . . P—B3 when the fight for control of the center will rage on. Prospects are even, with chances for both sides.

SICILIAN DEFENSE

Like the French Defense, the Sicilian Defense immediately puts a veto on White's intended choice of opening. The characteristic 1 . . . P—QB4 is more aggressive than the French, and also riskier. If you like a complicated game with chances for both sides, the Sicilian is an ideal defense.

An important point to remember is this: White generally plays an early P—Q4 in order to get more space for his pieces in the center. After Black captures White's Queen Pawn with his Queen Bishop Pawn, the Queen Bishop file is half open (from Black's side). By playing his Queen Rook— and sometimes his Queen as well—to the Queen Bishop file, Black can often exert considerable pressure along the file.

On the other hand, White has an important attacking motif in advancing his King Bishop Pawn: P—KB4. This often gives him a powerful position in the middle game, when he threatens P—K5 or P—B5.

(*a*) Dragon Variation

WHITE	BLACK		WHITE	BLACK
1 P—K4	P—QB4		4 NxP	N—B3
2 N—KB3	N—QB3		5 N—QB3	P—Q3
3 P—Q4	PxP		6 B—K2	. . . .

If 6 B—K3, P—KN3; 7 Q—Q2, B—N2; 8 Castles, Castles; 9 B—K2 intending a Pawn-storming attack on the King-side. However, after 9 . . . NxN; 10 BxN, Q—R4 Black has good counterplay.

6	P—KN3		7 B—K3	B—N2
	8 Castles	Castles		

Here the simplifying move 8 . . . N—KN5? looks tempting, for if 9 BxN, BxB; 10 QxB?, NxN and Black holds his own. But instead White plays 10 NxN! and no matter how Black replies, he loses a piece.

9 N—N3   B—K3   10 P—B4   Q—B1!

Chiefly played to prevent P—B5, which may lead to troublesome complications. Thus after the alternative 10 . . . N—QR4 there might follow 11 P—B5, B—B5; 12 NxN, BxB; 13 QxB, QxN; 14 P—KN4!, N—Q2; 15 N—Q5! and White has a strong initiative.

62

(Position after 10 . . . Q—B1!)

If White plays 11 P—KR3 (intending P—KN4 and P—B5), Black counters energetically with 11 . . . R—Q1! Then if 12 P—N4, P—Q4! or 12 B—B3, B—B5!

Black has a solid position with good prospects for the middle game. Note that his fianchettoed Bishop exerts strong pressure along the long diagonal.

(*b*) Scheveningen Variation

	WHITE	BLACK		WHITE	BLACK
1	P—K4	P—QB4	4	NxP	N—B3
2	N—KB3	N—QB3	5	N—QB3	P—Q3
3	P—Q4	PxP	6	B—K2	P—K3
			7	Castles	P—QR3

63

(Position after 7 . . . P—QR3)

Compare this Pawn formation with the one in Diagram 62. Black's Bishops have very little scope.

Aside from the following line, White can also proceed with 8 B—K3, Q—B2; 9 P—B4, B—K2; 10 N—N3, P—QN4; 11 B—B3, B—N2; 12 Q—K1! followed by Q—N3 with a strong attacking formation.

	WHITE	BLACK		WHITE	BLACK
8	K—R1	Q—B2	11	P—KN4!	B—Q2
9	P—B4	B—K2	12	P—N5	N—K1
10	B—B3	Castles	13	P—QR4	N—R4

White continues 14 P—B5! with a powerful initiative, thanks to the advance of his King-side Pawns. Black's position is constricted and limited to purely passive defense.

(*c*) 2 . . . P—K3 Variation

	WHITE	BLACK		WHITE	BLACK
1	P—K4	P—QB4	3	P—Q4	PxP
2	N—KB3	P—K3	4	NxP	N—KB3
			5	N—QB3	. . . .

64

(Position after 5 N—QB3)

Black's position is difficult. If he plays 5 . . . B—N5 there follows 6 P—K5!, N—Q4; 7 B—Q2, NxN; 8 PxN, B—K2; 9 Q—N4 with an aggressive position for White.

5	N—B3	6 N/Q4—N5	....

Black's game remains difficult because of the early advance of his King Pawn. If Black tries to prevent N—Q6ch with 6 . . . P—Q3, the reply 7 B—KB4 is embarrassing: note that 7 . . . N—K4? is wrong because of 8 Q—Q4! winning a Pawn, while if 7 . . . P—K4; 8 B—N5 and Black has a bad "hole" at his Queen 4 square.

6	B—N5	9 PxP	PxP
7 P—QR3	BxNch	10 B—Q3	Castles
8 NxB	P—Q4	11 Castles	....

White's position is definitely more promising. His two Bishops are a distinct asset for the endgame, and Black's isolated Queen Pawn is just as distinct a liability in an ending.

(d) 2 . . . N—KB3 Variation

WHITE	BLACK		WHITE	BLACK
1 P—K4	P—QB4		2 N—KB3	N—KB3
	3 P—K5	N—Q4		

65

(Position after 3 . . . N—Q4)

This line of play is a forerunner of Alekhine's Defense—see page 84. Black allows his King Knight to be driven away in the hope that White's King Pawn will be weakened by advancing—a futile hope.

4 P—Q4!	PxP	6 B—QB4!	N—QB3
5 QxP!	P—K3	7 Q—K4	N—N3

This is one opening line in which an early development of the Queen does no harm, as White's Queen has a commanding position and Black's development is backward.

8 B—N3	N—R4	10 RPxN	P—Q4
9 N—B3	NxB	11 PxP e.p.	BxP

White has superior development and open lines. Here is one likely way for him to gain the initiative: 12 Castles, Castles; 13 R—Q1, Q—K2; 14 N—QN5!, B—N1; 15 B—K3 and White must win a Pawn (his chief threat is 16 BxN).

(e) 2 N—QB3 Variation

WHITE	BLACK	WHITE	BLACK
1 P—K4	P—QB4	3 P—KN3	P—KN3
2 N—QB3	N—QB3	4 B—N2	B—N2

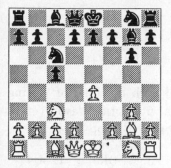

66

(Position after 4 ... B—N2)

White deliberately keeps the game closed, avoiding P—Q4. He trusts to superior maneuvering ability to obtain an advantage. However, with careful play Black maintains equality.

5 P—Q3	P—K3!	6 B—K3	Q—R4!

More promising than 6 ... N—Q5; 7 QN—K2! with a view to dislodging the advanced Knight by P—QB3. (If 7 ... NxN; 8 NxN, BxP; 9 QR—N1, Q—R4ch; 10 B—Q2, QxP; 11 RxB!, QxR; 12 B—QB3!)

7 KN—K2	N—Q5	9 N—B1	Castles
8 Q—Q2	N—K2	10 Castles	P—Q3

Even game. Black has done well to centralize his powerful Queen Knight, supported directly by the fianchettoed Bishop. White must play for King-side attack by P—B4 etc.

(f) Wing Gambit

WHITE	BLACK		WHITE	BLACK
1 P—K4	P—QB4		2 P—QN4	....

This is the Wing Gambit, played with the idea of getting a big lead in development and a powerful Pawn center (through the removal of Black's Queen Bishop Pawn).

| 2 .... | PxP | | 3 P—QR3 | P—Q4! |

Energetic counterplay in the center is the key to Black's policy against the gambit. White's reply is virtually forced, for after 4 P—K5?, N—QB3; 5 P—Q4, Q—B2; 6 N—KB3, B—N5 Black has a positional as well as material advantage.

| 4 KPxP | QxP | | 5 N—KB3 | .... |

Black was threatening 5 ... Q—K4ch.

| 5 .... | P—K4 | | 6 PxP | BxP |

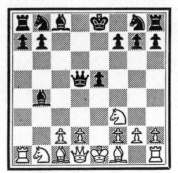

67
(Position after 6 ... BxP)

The gambit has turned out to be a miserable failure, for Black is ahead in development as well as material!

Black is well prepared for complications, for example 7 N—R3, B—Q2!; 8 N—B4, N—QB3!, 9 N—N6, Q—K5ch; 10 B—K2, R—Q1 with a very good game. Or 7 N—R3, B—Q2!; 8 B—N2, N—QB3; 9 N—QN5, R—B1!; 10 NxRP, NxN; 11 RxN, P—K5!; 12 BxP, PxN; 13 PxP, B—QB4! with a winning attack.

7 P—B3	B—QB4	9 N—QN5	Castles!
8 N—R3	N—KB3	10 B—K2	....

Note that 10 N—B7 is answered by 10 . . . BxPch!

10	P—K5!	12 N—B7	Q—N4
11 KN—Q4	N—B3	13 NxR	....

Or 13 NxN, QxP; 14 R—B1, PxN; 15 NxR, N—N5 and Black must win.

13	QxP	14 R—B1	N—K4

Black has a winning attack, for example 15 P—Q3, B—KR6; 16 PxP, NxP etc.

CARO-KANN DEFENSE

Like the French Defense, the Caro-Kann Defense (1 P—K4, P—QB3) allows White to build a broad Pawn center and then challenges that center with 2 ... P—Q4. But, since Black plays 1 ... P—QB3 instead of 1 ... P—K3, it follows that in most variations his Queen Bishop is not imprisoned.

This is definitely a defense for players who want a solid, even position with little chance of complications. A player who wants to avoid risks and who is satisfied with a draw, should favor this defense.

(*a*) 3 N—QB3 Variation with 4 ... B—B4.

WHITE	BLACK	WHITE	BLACK
1 P—K4	P—QB3	2 P—Q4	P—Q4

Note that White has little to gain from 3 P—K5, B—B4! for example 4 B—Q3, BxB; 5 QxB, P—K3; 6 N—KB3, Q—N3; 7 Castles, P—QB4 etc.

3 N—QB3	PxP	6 N—B3	N—Q2
4 NxP	B—B4	7 P—KR4	P—KR3
5 N—N3	B—N3	8 B—Q3	....

68

(Position after 8 B—Q3)

White has decided to exchange Bishops, as Black's Queen Bishop was too well posted. The exchange increases White's lead in development and gains time for castling on the Queen-side.

8	BxB	11 Castles QR	Q—B2
9 QxB	P—K3	12 K—N1	Castles
10 B—Q2	KN—B3	13 P—B4!	P—B4

White continues 14 B—B3! with distinctly more freedom for his pieces and strong pressure on the center. However, Black has no weak points and is well equipped for careful defense.

(*b*)   3 N—QB3 Variation with 4 . . . N—B3

WHITE	BLACK	WHITE	BLACK
1 P—K4	P—QB3	3 N—QB3	PxP
2 P—Q4	P—Q4	4 NxP	N—B3
	5 NxNch	....	

69

(Position after 5 NxNch)

Whichever way Black captures he remains with a theoretical disadvantage, as his doubled Pawn is a positional weakness. White, on the other hand, has a clear majority of Pawns . on the Queen-side, which will eventually be converted into a passed Pawn.

5	KPxN

Or 5 . . . NPxN; 6 N—K2! with a favorable setup for White, for example 6 . . . B—B4; 7 N—N3, B—N3; 8 P—KR4, P—KR3; 9 P—R5, B—R2; 10 P—QB3, Q—N3; 11 B—QB4 etc.

6 N—B3	B—KN5	10 R—K1	N—Q2
7 B—K2	B—Q3	11 B—Q2	Q—B2
8 Castles	Castles	12 P—KR3!	B—R4
9 P—B4!	R—K1	13 B—B3!	....

White has greater command of the board and his potential passed Pawn (after an eventual P—Q5) gives him a marked positional advantage.

(c)   3 N—QB3 Variation with 4 ... N—Q2

WHITE	BLACK	WHITE	BLACK
1 P—K4	P—QB3	4 NxP	N—Q2
2 P—Q4	P—Q4	5 N—KB3	KN—B3
3 N—QB3	PxP	6 N—N3	P—K3

70

(Position after 6 ... P—K3)

By avoiding 4 ... N—B3 Black has eliminated the possibility of getting a doubled Pawn. However, his position shows signs of becoming unpleasantly constricted. (His Queen Bishop has no move!)

7 B—Q3	B—Q3	9 Q—K2	Q—B2
8 Castles	Castles	10 N—K4	B—B5

White's development has been more efficient and he has more room for his pieces.

(*d*) 4 P—QB4 Variation

WHITE	BLACK		WHITE	BLACK
1 P—K4	P—QB3		3 PxP	PxP
2 P—Q4	P—Q4		4 P—QB4	....

Note that 4 B—Q3, N—QB3; 5 P—QB3, N—B3; 6 B—KB4, P—KN3; 7 N—B3, B—N2 gives Black an easy game.

4	N—KB3		5 N—QB3	N—B3

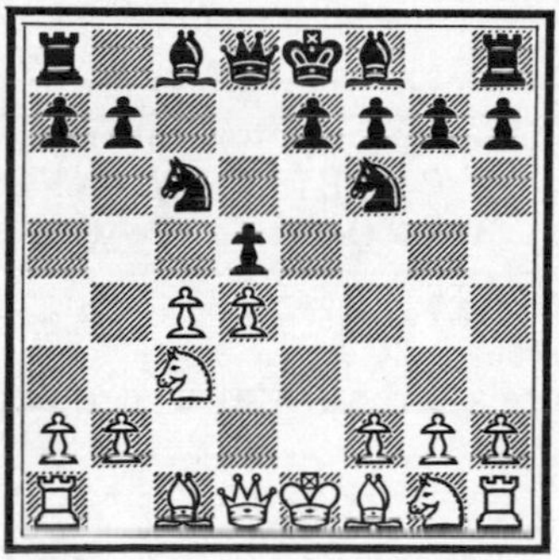

71

(Position after 5 . . . N—B3)

White's only hope for initiative is to put more pressure on the center—hence 6 B—N5 — but Black can parry adequately.

6 B—N5	P—K3		9 R—B1	N—K5!
7 N—B3	B—K2		10 BxB	QxB
8 P—B5	Castles		11 B—K2	R—Q1!

Black has equal prospects, as he is able to free himself after 12 Castles with 12 . . . P—K4!

This vehement counterattack is considered premature, as it leads to a difficult game for Black. After 1 P—K4, Black plays the dashing 1 . . . N—KB3. The idea is to provoke the advance of White's center Pawns to the point where they become weak. Actual practice has not borne out this attractive theory, and therefore this defense is best avoided in favor of some more solid line of play.

(*a*) Four Pawns' Variation

WHITE	BLACK		WHITE	BLACK
1 P—K4	N—KB3		3 P—QB4	N—N3
2 P—K5	N—Q4		4 P—Q4	P—Q3
	5 P—B4		PxP	

Black hopes to undermine White's broad Pawn center. The attempt is destined to fail.

6 BPxP	N—B3		9 N—B3	Q—Q2
7 B—K3	B—B4		10 B—K2	Castles
8 N—QB3	P—K3		11 Castles	....

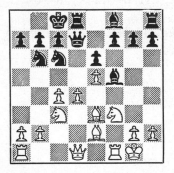

72

(Position after 11 Castles)

The indicated Pawn push 12 P—Q5 has tremendous power, for example 11 . . . B—K2; 12 P—Q5!, PxP; 13 BxN, RPxB; 14 PxP, N—N5; 15 N—Q4!, P—N3; 16 NxB, PxN; 17 RxP!, NxQP (if 17 . . . QxR; 18 B—N4); 18 P—K6!!, PxP; 19 RxN!, PxR; 20 B—N4 winning.

11	P—B3		14 BxN	NxNch
12 PxP	PxP		15 BxN!	RPxB
13 P—Q5!	N—K4		16 N—N5	....

White has a winning attack with Q—R4. He has taken energetic advantage of the poor position of Black's pieces.

(*b*) Three Pawns' Variation

WHITE	BLACK		WHITE	BLACK
1 P—K4	N—KB3		3 P—QB4	N—N3
2 P—K5	N—Q4		4 P—Q4	P—Q3

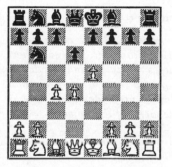

73

(Position after 4 . . . P—Q3)

Now White decides to exchange Pawns—a less aggressive but safer course than the one he followed in the previous variation.

5 PxP   KPxP

Here 5 . . . BPxP is definitely inferior: 6 P—Q5!, P—KN3; 7 B—K3!, B—N2; 8 B—Q4! and the removal of the valuable fianchettoed Bishop breaks the spine of Black's position.

6 N—QB3	N—B3		9 KN—K2!	B—N5
7 B—K3	B—K2		10 Castles	R—K1
8 B—Q3	Castles		11 P—KR3	B—R4

White continues 12 Q—Q2, remaining with a freer and more promising position.

(c)   4 N—KB3 Variation

	WHITE	BLACK		WHITE	BLACK
1	P—K4	N—KB3	3	P—Q4	P—Q3
2	P—K5	N—Q4	4	N—KB3	. . . .

74
(Position after 4 N—KB3)

In this variation, White concentrates on quiet development. However, here too Black's King Knight ends up poorly posted at Queen Knight 3. This placement is definitely one of the drawbacks of the defense.

4	....	B—N5	8	PxP	PxP
5	B—K2	N—QB3	9	P—QN3	B—K2
6	Castles	P—K3	10	B—K3	Castles
7	P—B4	N—N3	11	N—B3	P—Q4

Otherwise P—Q5 drives the Queen Knight away.

12	P—B5	N—Q2	13	P—QN4!	....

With his Queen-side majority of Pawns White has a decided positional advantage. If Black tries 13 . . . NxNP then 14 R—N1 recovers the Pawn and leaves White with an even greater advantage—a passed Queen Bishop Pawn.

CENTER COUNTER DEFENSE

This is definitely an inferior defense. The early moves of Black's Queen lose time, with further loss of time indicated. This comes about because after 1 P—K4, Black replies 1 ... P—Q4 instead of preparing this Pawn move with 1 ... P—K3 (French Defense) or with 1 ... P—QB3 (Caro-Kann Defense).

WHITE	BLACK	WHITE	BLACK
1 P—K4	P—Q4	2 PxP	QxP
3 N—QB3		Q—QR4	

75

(Position after 3 ... Q—QR4)

Black's faulty development of the Queen has allowed White to gain time for his own development. Later on, White will gain more time by further attacks on the Black Queen.

4 P—Q4	N—KB3

Another possibility is 4 ... P—K4; 5 PxP, QxKPch; 6 B—K2 followed by 7 N—B3 driving away the Black Queen with gain of time.

5 N—B3	B—N5	6 P—KR3!	B—R4

Or 6 ... BxN; 7 QxB and White remains ahead in development and also has the positional advantage of two Bishops against Bishop and Knight.

| 7 P—KN4! | B—N3 | 8 N—K5! | P—B3 |

Preparing a retreat for his Queen in view of the threat of N—B4.

| 9 P—KR4! | N—K5 | 10 B—Q2 | Q—N3 |

Even worse is 10 . . . NxB; 11 QxN (threatening to win a piece with P—R5), P—B3; 12 NxB, PxN; 13 B—Q3 when Black's King-side Pawn formation has been damaged irreparably.

| 11 NxB | NxN | 13 Q—Q2 | P—K3 |
| 12 BxN | RPxN | 14 Castles | . . . . |

White continues 15 B—N2, and with his greater freedom of action and his two Bishops against Bishop and Knight, has a clear positional advantage. Black's game has no compensating features.

NIMZOVICH DEFENSE

This is another mediocre defense that has little to recommend it. The immediate development of Black's Queen Knight (1 . . . N—QB3 in answer to 1 P—K4) is untimely, and generally leaves White with a substantial lead in development.

(a) 2 . . . P—Q4 Variation

WHITE	BLACK		WHITE	BLACK
1 P—K4	N—QB3		2 P—Q4	P—Q4

76

(Position after 2 . . . P—Q4)

White can now push by with 3 P—K5, but this allows Black to develop comfortably with 3 . . . B—B4. Hence White prefers to try a different way.

3 N—QB3	P—K3

After 3 . . . PxP, White disrupts his opponent's position with 4 P—Q5! Then on 4 . . . N—K4 he can either stop to regain his Pawn, or else play a gambit for rapid development with 5 P—B3!

WHITE	BLACK		WHITE	BLACK
4 N—B3	B—N5		5 P—K5	BxNch
6 PxB	N—R4			

Now White has excellent attacking prospects.

7 P—QR4	N—K2	10 Q—N4	P—B5
8 B—Q3	P—QN3	11 B—K2	N—B4
9 N—Q2!	P—QB4	12 N—B3	....

White has all the play and a clear initiative. His Queen Bishop can take up a strong position at Queen Rook 3.

(*b*) 2 ... P—K4 Variation·

WHITE	BLACK		WHITE	BLACK
1 P—K4	N—QB3		3 PxP	NxP
2 P—Q4	P—K4		4 N—QB3	B—B4

Another way is 4 . . . N—KB3, after which White gets the upper hand with 5 P—B4, N—B3; 6 P—K5, N—KN1; 7 N—B3, P—Q3; 8 B—N5 etc.

5 P—B4	N—N3		8 Q—K2	BxB
6 N—B3	P—Q3		9 QxB	Q—Q2
7 B—B4	B—K3		10 P—B5	....

White's pieces are actively posted and his position holds out great promise. Black's forces are scattered and no good plan of development is available.

YUGOSLAV DEFENSE

This line of play (1 . . . P—Q3 in reply to 1 P—K4) is as timid as Alekhine's Defense is brash. White maintains clear superiority by virtue of his better development and greater command of the board.

WHITE	BLACK		WHITE	BLACK
1 P—K4	P—Q3		2 P—Q4	N—KB3

77

(Position after 2 . . . N—KB3)

Black counterattacks against White's King Pawn, which cannot very well advance. Consequently White protects the menaced Pawn.

3 N—QB3	P—KN3		5 N—B3	Castles
4 P—B4!	B—N2		6 B—Q3	P—B4

Black makes a flank thrust against White's formidable Pawn center.

7 P—Q5	P—K3		9 P—B5!	B—B1
8 PxP	BxP		10 Castles	N—B3

White's development is much more active and aggressive. Particularly troublesome is his threat to obtain a lasting bind with B—KN5 followed by N—Q5. Black is limited to passive play.

THE QUEEN PAWN OPENINGS

While the Queen's Gambit is mentioned in fifteenth-century manuscripts, for centuries it was outside the mainstream of accepted and popular play. Its wide adoption dates only from the turn of the century and, at that, probably 90 per cent of the currently used variations date from the 1920's or later.

As for the other chief openings we find in this section — Nimzoindian Defense, King's Indian Defense, Gruenfeld Defense, and Queen's Indian Defense — as late as 1920 they were adopted only sporadically. Even after that date they were often nameless, being dismissed with the patronizing title, "Irregular Defense."

Since that time these openings have crystallized as independent lines of play. Each one has its distinctive character and its special problems. Each is firmly established in the opening repertoire, so that a knowledge of the basic ideas and possibilities is essential to every player of every grade of skill. The following survey has been assembled to meet that need.

QUEEN'S GAMBIT

Since the turn of the century this opening, beginning with 1 P—Q4, has been the favorite line of play used by the masters. It is much less popular among average players, who have some psychological difficulties with it. When they have White, they do not care to play 1 P—Q4. Yet when they have Black, they are exceedingly uncomfortable when their opponent starts with 1 P—Q4.

Consequently the Queen's Gambit is a formidable weapon, both technically and psychologically. The player who is reasonably familiar with its fine points has a marked advantage over his rivals.

What makes the Queen's Gambit such a dreaded weapon is that White often obtains much greater freedom of action for his pieces. As a result, he gets a frequently decisive command of the board. Sometimes this takes the form of slow strangulation of Black's forces; sometimes, through his superior mobility, White is able to win by extraordinarily brilliant play.

This explains why most players are afraid to play Black against the gambit. They either know from dreadful experience or from the reputation of this opening that they are about to confront a very trying ordeal. Yet, as has been explained, these same players, when they have White, will avoid playing the Queen's Gambit! Rightly or wrongly, they feel they do not know enough about it.

The Queen's Gambit starts with these moves:

1 P—Q4   P—Q4   2 P—QB4   . . . .

78

(Position after 2 P—QB4)

White threatens to obtain an over-whelming Pawn center with PxP. If Black plays 2 . . . PxP, White may still very well obtain the overwhelming Pawn center.

White's offer of a Pawn by 2 P—QB4 constitutes the Queen's Gambit. A gambit, as you know, is an opening in which material is offered speculatively for the purpose of gaining development or other advantages. The King Pawn opening gambits, such as the King's Gambit or the Evans Gambit, have a highly speculative character. The Queen's Gambit, in most forms, is less of a gamble, as White can generally recover the Pawn with ease. (For example, if Black plays 2 . . . PxP, White can recover the Pawn immediately with 3 Q—R4ch if he wants to.)

Thus we see that there is little about this gambit that can be called speculative. On the other hand, 2 P—QB4 embodies a definite threat. *White is momentarily threatening to remove Black's center Pawn.* If he gets rid of Black's Queen Pawn, White can soon continue with P—K4, obtaining a broad Pawn center and leaving Black with a hopeless inferiority in space. (White, in the position of Diagram 78, threatens 3 PxP, QxP; 4 N—QB3 followed by 5 P—K4 with an over-whelming position.)

Our main problem is: *how is Black to maintain a firm*

foothold in the center? To maintain a hold in the center is essential for Black. If he loses out in the center, he will be faced with the danger of White's getting overwhelming control of the board. (This is exactly what happens when Black is not familiar with the pitfalls of this opening.)

The object of our treatment of this vital opening is to familiarize you with the basic schemes that must be followed by White and Black. You will see what White aims for, and how Black parries the dangers involved. After you read this section, you should be able to play the Queen's Gambit Declined for either side, with a fair amount of confidence.

QUEEN'S GAMBIT DECLINED

2 . . . P—K3 Defense

To ensure his hold on the center, Black must support his Queen Pawn *with a Pawn move.* Then, if White plays PxP, Black replies . . . PxP. In this way he keeps a Pawn at his Queen 4 square and maintains a solid foothold in the center.

Black has two supporting Pawn moves that will answer the purpose: 2 . . . P—K3 (treated in this section) and 2 . . . P—QB3 (see page 113ff.).

So let us see the consequences of 2 . . . P—K3.

2 . . . .   P—K3

79

(Position after 2 . . . P—K3)

Black now has a firm foothold in the center, but a new problem has arisen for him: how is he to develop his Queen Bishop?

By playing . . . P—K3, Black has blocked the diagonal of his Queen Bishop. This piece is solidly hemmed in by the Black Pawn at King 3, which is why the Bishop is sometimes known as "the problem child of the Queen's Gambit."

It is this serious loss of mobility which often leads to defeat for Black. If he fails to bring out the Bishop, his development remains inadequate for the rest of the game, giving White an advantage which often reaches right down into the ending. Worse yet, many a player of the Black pieces is not even aware of this danger!

However, since we do see the problem, how are we to solve it? There are two possible ways: (a) to strive for . . . P—K4, which will open the Queen Bishop's diagonal, or (b) to fianchetto this Bishop by playing . . . P—QN3 or . . . P—QN4. These, then, are generally Black's objectives. Where he fails to achieve them, his Queen Bishop's lack of mobility may often lose the game for him.

Diagram 3 shows the consequences of Black's failing to solve the problem of the Queen Bishop.

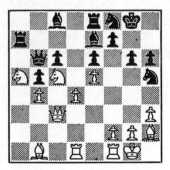

80

No matter how Black turns and squirms, he cannot develop his Queen Bishop. It is hemmed in in all directions by Black Pawns on white squares (his King Pawn, Queen Bishop Pawn, Queen Knight Pawn).

When we turn to specific variations, we find that they revolve to a considerable extent about this problem. But White has other trumps that Black must watch out for.

Thus, White can often post his King Knight on his King 5

square very effectively. Here the Knight has a magnificent center outpost, radiating power in all directions. An example of this is seen in Diagram 81. White's Queen, Knight, and Bishop aim powerfully at the King-side, while his Rook on Queen Bishop 3 is poised for R—KR3 or R—KN3.

81

If Black tries 1 . . . N—Q2 (to get rid of White's Knight), the sequel might be 2 R—KR3, P—KR3; 3 RxP!!, PxR; 4 Q—N3ch, K—R1; 5 N—N6ch!, PxN; 6 QxQ. Or 3 . . . P—B3; 4 R—R8ch!!, KxR; 5 Q— R4ch, K—N1; 6 Q—R7 mate.

Another danger (partly illustrated in the play arising from Diagram 81) is that White's King Bishop can operate formidably on the diagonal Queen Knight 1 to King Rook 7, leading to the heart of Black's castled position. This menace becomes even more drastic if White's Queen is on the same diagonal, as in Diagram 82.

82

White plays 1 B—N1 (with the threat of 2 BxN, BxB; 3 QxP mate). Black stops this with 1 . . . P—N3, but there follows 2 BxN, BxB; 3 N—K4!, B— K2; 4 P—QN4! and White wins a piece.

Finally, you must remember that White's second move

in the Queen's Gambit Declined (2 P—QB4) often allows him to open the Queen Bishop file and post his Queen Rook powerfully on it. (An example of this appears on page 101.) Black must be in a position to neutralize this pressure, and the best way for him to do it is to aim for a fairly early ... P—QB4, assuring himself counterplay for his own Rooks on the Queen Bishop file.

Thus you see that the dangers Black must meet are many, varied, and formidable. Yet there is no reason to despair. If Black is unaware of the dangers, there is a strong likelihood that he will succumb to them. If he is aware of them, however, he can take countermeasures in good time.

(a) Orthodox Defense

| 1 P—Q4 | P—Q4 | 2 P—QB4 | P—K3 |

Now White has the choice of bringing out his Queen Knight or King Knight. 3 N—KB3 is less exact, as it may lead to Variations (e), (f), or (g), which give Black an easier game than after 3 N—QB3.

| 3 N—QB3 | N—KB3 | 4 B—N5 | .... |

83

(Position after 4 B—N5)

By now playing 4 ... QN—Q2, Black sets one of the most popular traps in the whole range of the openings: 5 PxP, PxP; 6 NxP??, NxN!!; 7 BxQ, B—N5ch; 8 Q—Q2, BxQch; 9 KxB, KxB and Black has won a piece!

4 ....   QN—Q2

It doesn't matter whether Black plays 4 . . . QN—Q2 or
4 . . . B—K2. But if he wishes to adopt the Cambridge
Springs Defense—Variation (c), he must play . . . QN—Q2.

5 P—K3   B—K2   6 N—B3   Castles
      7 R—B1!   ....

The Rook move exercises a powerful restraining grip on
Black's game. It sets up the potential pressure of the Rook
on the Queen Bishop file.

7 ....   P—B3

Temporarily neutralizing the pressure of White's Rook
along the Queen Bishop file. Of course, Black still means to
play ... P—B4 at a suitable moment later on.

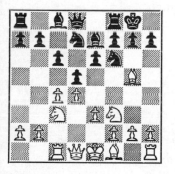

84

(Position after 7 . . . P—B3)

*Black must think hard about the
problem of developing his Queen
Bishop. Note that at this moment the
Bishop does not have a single move!*

8 B—Q3   ....

This is a crucial position, and Black can easily go wrong.
In one game, for example, the play was 8 . . . P—QN3?;
9 PxP, NxP; 10 NxN, BPxN; 11 BxB, QxB; 12 R—B7!,
Q—N5ch; 13 Q—Q2, QxQch; 14 KxQ, P—QR3; 15 KR—
QB1 and White has a strategically won game.

Nor is the preparation for fianchettoing Black's Queen Bishop fully successful: 8 . . . P—KR3; 9 B—R4, PxP; 10 BxP, P—QN4; 11 B—Q3, P—R3; 12 Castles, P—B4; 13 P—R4! (this forces a weakening of Black's Queen-side Pawns), P—B5; 14 B—N1, N—Q4; 15 BxB, QxB; 16 P—QN3! and Black ends up with a weak Pawn on the Queen-side.

| 8 .... | PxP | 9 BxBP | N—Q4 |

Black has surrendered the center in order to free his constricted position by several exchanges—and also in the hope of freeing his imprisoned Bishop.

| 10 BxB | QxB | 11 Castles | .... |

White can avoid the exchange of Knights with 11 N—K4, but after 11 . . . KN—B3; 12 N—N3, P—K4! (freedom for the Bishop!) Black stands well enough.

| 11 .... | NxN | 12 RxN | P—K4 |

85

(Position after 12 . . . P—K4)

At last Black has made the liberating move . . . P—K4, which means that the development of his Bishop is assured.

In the event of 13 PxP, NxP; 14 NxN, QxN; 15 P—B4 Black can hold his own with 15 . . . Q—K5!; 16 B—N3, B—B4!; 17 Q—R5, P—KN3; 18 Q—R6, QR—Q1 etc.

13 Q—N1!   . . . .

With this move White continues to maintain some advantage in space. If now 13 . . . P—K5; 14 N—Q2, N—B3; 15 P—QN4!, P—QR3; 16 KR—B1, B—N5; 17 P—QR4 and White has strong play on the Queen Bishop file with the coming P—N5 etc.

Probably best for Black is 13 . . . PxP; 14 PxP, N—N3; 15 B—N3, Q—B3; 16 R—K1, B—K3; 17 BxB, PxB; 18 R/B3—K3, QR—K1. *White still has more space for his pieces, but Black has completed his development and has a strong point for his Knight at Queen 4.*

(b) Exchange Variation

1 P—Q4	P—Q4		4 B—N5	QN—Q2
2 P—QB4	P—K3		5 P—K3	P—B3
3 N—QB3	N—KB3		6 PxP	KPxP

It will become clear later on that White is pursuing a definite policy with this exchange of Pawns, despite the fact that the swap allows Black to open the diagonal for his Queen Bishop.

7 B—Q3   B—K2

Planning to free his game with 8 . . . N—K5!

8 Q—B2!   . . . .

86

(Position after 8 Q—B2!)

White's last move has prevented 8 . . . N—K5? which would now be answered by 9 BxB winning a Pawn. So Black must find some other way to free himself.

White plans to play QR—N1 in due course, followed by P—QN4 and P—N5. If Black then exchanges Pawns (. . . BPxNP) he is left with a weak Queen Pawn and Queen Knight Pawn; aside from which, White has the mastery of the open Queen Bishop file.

On the other hand, if Black stands pat against this "minority attack" and allows White to play NPxBP, then Black is left with a backward Queen Bishop Pawn on the open Queen Bishop file. Such a Pawn remains a lasting weakness right into the endgame stage.

Here are some typical possibilities: 8 . . . N—R4; 9 BxB, QxB; 10 KN—K2, P—KN3; 11 Castles KR, P—KB4; 12 QR—N1, Castles; 13 P—QN4!, P—QR3; 14 P—QR4, P—B5! (counterplay on the King-side); 15 NxBP, NxN; 16 PxN, RxP; 17 N—K2, R—B3; 18 P—N5, RPxP; 19 PxP, N—B1; 20 PxP, PxP. Black is left with the backward Queen Bishop Pawn.

Or 8 . . . N—B1; 9 N—B3, N—K3; 10 B—R4, P—KN3; 11 Castles KR, Castles; 12 QR—N1, N—N2; 13 P—QN4!, B—B4 (getting rid of the problem child); 14 P—N5, BxB; 15 QxB, N—B4; 16 PxP, NxB; 17 NxN, PxP. Again Black is left with the backward Queen Bishop Pawn.

| 8 .... | Castles | 9 N—B3 | R—K1 |
| | 10 Castles KR | .... | |

Now it is still too soon for 10 . . . N—K5? for then 11 BxN! wins a Pawn. (Black's King Rook Pawn is unprotected.)

| 10 .... | N—B1 | 11 QR—N1 | N—K5 |

If now 12 BxN, BxB and Black is safe. (His King Rook Pawn is protected.)

| | 12 BxB | QxB |

87

(Position after 12 . . . QxB)

Again White is in a position to carry out the minority attack: 13 P—QN4!, P—QR3; 14 P—QR4, NxN; 15 QxN followed eventually by P—N5 with a strong initiative.

(c) Cambridge Springs Defense

| 1 P—Q4 | P—Q4 | 3 N—QB3 | N—KB3 |
| 2 P—QB4 | P—K3 | 4 B—N5 | QN—Q2 |

A good alternative is 4 . . . B—N5, with ideas akin to those of the Nimzoindian Defense (page 132).

After 4 . . . QN—Q2, White can, if he wishes, transpose into the Exchange Variation with 5 or 6 PxP.

| 5 P—K3 | P—B3 | 6 N—B3 | Q—R4 |

88

(Position after 6 . . . Q—R4)

With his last move Black pins White's Queen Knight, exploiting the absence of White's Queen Bishop. Note that 7 PxP is not so good now, as Black has 7 . . . NxP, intensifying the pin.

7 N—Q2   . . . .

Taking measures against the pin. Black can now get equality with 7 . . . B—N5; 8 Q—B2, PxP (attacking White's Queen Bishop); 9 BxN, NxB; 10 NxP, BxNch; 11 QxB, QxQch; 12 PxQ, K—K2; 13 P—B3, B—Q2; 14 QR—N1, P—QN3; 15 N—K5, KR—QB1 followed by . . . P—B4. However, the main line is even simpler and more promising.

7	PxP	10 R—B1	N—Q4!
8 BxN	NxB	11 B—Q3	NxN
9 NxP	Q—B2	12 PxN	. . . .

Not 12 RxN?, B—N5 winning the Exchange.

12	B—K2	14 P—B4	P—KN3
13 Castles	Castles	15 N—K5	P—QB4

The position is approximately even. White has a freer game, but Black's Bishop-pair has great potential power.

(d) Lasker's Defense

1 P—Q4	P—Q4	5 P—K3	Castles
2 P—QB4	P—K3	6 N—B3	P—KR3
3 N—QB3	N—KB3	7 B—R4	N—K5!
4 B—N5	B—K2	8 BxB	QxB

89

(Position after 8 . . . QxB)

Black's emphasis is on exchanging and simplifying so as to liberate his remaining forces.

Black has already achieved a satisfactory position, for example 9 NxN, PxN; 10 N—Q2, P—K4! Then if 11 NxP?, PxP; 12 QxP??, R—Q1 and Black wins a piece.

Or if 9 Q—B2, NxN; 10 QxN, PxP!; 11 BxP, P—QN3!; 12 Castles KR, B—N2; 13 B—K2, R—B1!; 14 KR—Q1, P—QB4! and Black stands well.

9 PxP	NxN	10 PxN	PxP

Black's Bishop is liberated at last.

11 Q—N3	R—Q1	13 BxP	N—B3
12 P—B4	PxP	14 Q—B3	B—N5

90

(Position after 14 . . . B—N5)

Black's Bishop has developed with a threat of 15 . . . BxN; 16 PxB, NxP (or 16 . . . RxP).

| 15 Castles KR | BxN | 16 PxB | Q—B3 |

Black has a thoroughly satisfactory position. All his pieces are in good play.

(e) Prague Variation

| 1 P—Q4 | P—Q4 | 3 N—QB3 | N—KB3 |
| 2 P—QB4 | P—K3 | 4 N—B3 | P—B4 |

Thanks to the fact that White's fourth move here is less energetic than 4 B—N5, Black can hit back vigorously in the center.

91

(Position after 4 . . . P—B4)

If now 5 B—N5, BPxP; 6 KNxP, P—K4; 7 N—B3, P—Q5; 8 N—Q5, B—K2; 9 NxB, QxN with a good game for Black.

| 5 BPxP | NxP! |

After 5 . . . KPxP Black would be faced with the later possibility of PxP, leaving him with an isolated Queen Pawn as in Variation (h).

6 P—K4	NxN	8 PxP	B—N5ch
7 PxN	PxP	9 B—Q2	BxBch

As in the previous variation, Black frees his game by exchanging pieces.

10 QxB	Castles	12 Castles KR	P—QN3
11 B—B4	N—B3	13 KR—Q1	B—N2

Black has developed his Queen Bishop satisfactorily. After 14 Q—B4, R—B1 he has a good game. White has a powerful-looking Pawn center, but Black has the Queen-side majority of Pawns. Both sides have good prospects for the middle game.

(f) Duras Variation

1 P—Q4	P—Q4	3 N—KB3	N—KB3
2 P—QB4	P—K3	4 B—N5	P—KR3!

This takes advantage of the fact that White's third move is not quite so strong as 3 N—QB3.

White's next move is practically forced, for if 5 B—R4, B—N5ch!; 6 N—B3, PxP! and Black can hold the gambit Pawn in all variations.

Proof: if 7 P—K4? P—KN4!, winning White's King Pawn (this is the point of 4 . . . P—KR3!). If 7 P—K3, P—QN4! (this is the point of 5 . . . B—N5ch!). Finally, if 7 Q—R4ch, N—B3; 8 P—QR3, BxNch; 9 PxB, Q—Q4!; 10 P—K3, P—QN4 and again Black keeps the Pawn.

5 BxN   QxB

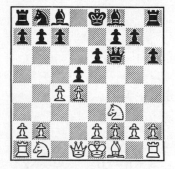

92

(Position after 5 . . . QxB)

Black has the positional advantage of two Bishops against Bishop and Knight; but his position is somewhat constricted.

6 Q—N3	P—B3		10 B—Q3	N—B3
7 QN—Q2	N—Q2		11 NxNch	QxN
8 P—K4	PxKP		12 Castles KR	B—Q3
9 NxP	Q—B5		13 KR—K1	Castles

Equal game. White has a freer position, but Black's forces have considerable potential power, especially if he can free his Queen Bishop.

(g) Vienna Variation

1 P—Q4	P—Q4		4 B—N5	B—N5ch
2 P—QB4	P—K3		5 N—B3	PxP
3 N—KB3	N—KB3		6 P—K4	P—B4

This counterthrust in the center leads to very exciting play. Here again Black has taken advantage of the fact that 3 N—KB3 is less energetic than 3 N—QB3.

An extremely complicated game can now arise from 7 P—K5, but it appears that Black can hold his own, for example 7 . . . PxP; 8 PxN, PxP; 9 Q—R4ch, N—B3; 10 Castles,

PxB; 11 NxQP, BxN!; 12 PxB, B—Q2!; 13 NxN, Q—B2!
etc. Or 7 . . . PxP; 8 Q—R4ch, N—B3; 9 Castles, B—Q2!;
10 N—K4, B—K2; 11 PxN, PxP; 12 B—R4, QR—B1!;
13 K—N1, N—R4; 14 Q—B2, P—K4! and Black has compensation for the piece down. (His Pawns are powerful.)

7 BxP   . . . .

Black can now play 7 . . . PxP; 8 NxP, BxNch; 9 PxB,
QN—Q2 with a perfectly safe game. However, 7 . . . PxP;
8 NxP, Q—R4 seems much too risky: 9 BxN!, BxNch; 10
PxB, QxBPch; 11 K—B1, QxBch; 12 K—N1, N—Q2 (not
12 . . . PxB?; 13 R—B1 winning); 13 R—B1!, Q—R3;
14 BxNP and White has a terrific initiative.

7 . . . .   BxNch!   8 PxB   Q—R4!

93

(Position after 8 . . . Q—R4!)

*Black must win a Pawn, for example
9 Q—B2 (or 9 Q—Q3), NxP! etc.
Or 9 BxN, QxBPch; 10 N—Q2, PxB;
11 PxP, N—Q2 etc.*

*This line of play is unsatisfactory for White, as Black wins
material.*

(h) Tarrasch Defense

1 P—Q4	P—Q4	3 N—QB3	P—QB4
2 P—QB4	P—K3	4 BPxP!	KPxP

White intends to burden Black with an isolated Queen Pawn (see White's ninth move).

5 N—B3   N—QB3   6 P—KN3!   . . . .

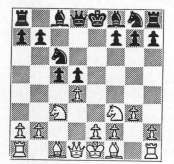

94

(Position after 6 P—KN3!)

White will fianchetto his King Bishop in order to exert powerful pressure on Black's weak Queen Pawn.

6 . . . .   N—B3   8 Castles   Castles
7 B—N2   B—K2   9 PxP!   . . . .

This is the move that sets off White's advantage. The counter gambit 9 . . . P—Q5 simply leaves Black a Pawn down after 10 N—QR4, B—B4; 11 B—B4, N—K5; 12 P—QN4!, B—B3; 13 P—N5, N—K2; 14 B—K5.

9 . . . .   BxP   11 B—K3   N—K5
10 N—QR4   B—K2   12 R—B1   . . . .

White has a marked positional advantage, thanks to Black's isolated Queen Pawn.

Summary: After 3 N—QB3, Black's most promising defenses appear to be the Cambridge Springs Defense, Lasker's Defense, and the Prague Variation.

After 3 N—KB3, Black does well with the Duras Variation or Vienna Variation.

SLAV DEFENSE

2 ... P—QB3

By propping up his Queen Pawn with 2 . . . P—QB3 Black takes up the fight for the center in the same way as when playing 2 . . . P—K3. However, 2 . . . P—QB3 does not block his Queen Bishop, and, as we would expect, we often see the Black Bishop developed to King Bishop 4 (or even to King Knight 5) in this line of play.

After 2 . . . P—QB3 Black frequently accepts the gambit on move 4, on the theory that he can fight for the center by playing his Queen Bishop to King Bishop 4. White generally gets the better of it, however, by angling for P—K4, or trying to control the center in some other fashion.

Despite the early . . . P—QB3, Black will generally try to free his game in the late opening or early middle game by playing . . . P—QB4.

The so called "Semi-Slav" defenses involve Black's playing . . . P—K3 after . . . P—QB3. As this hems in his Queen Bishop, he will generally try to fianchetto his problem Bishop.

(a) Deferred Acceptance of the Gambit

1 P—Q4	P—Q4	3 N—KB3	N—B3
2 P—QB4	P—QB3	4 N—B3	PxP

Here 4 . . . B—B4 looks *logical*, but after 5 PxP!, PxP; 6 Q—N3! Black is in trouble because of the twofold attack on his Queen Knight Pawn and Queen Pawn.

After 4 . . . PxP White can play to recover the gambit Pawn directly by 5 P—K3, P—QN4; 6 P—QR4, P—N5 (if 6 . . . P—QR3; 7 PxP, BPxP; 8 NxP etc.); 7 N—R2, P—K3;

8 BxP etc. But as this leaves his Queen Knight out of the game, White chooses a different way.

5 P—QR4   B—B4

95

(Position after 5 . . . B—B4)

Black has achieved his heart's desire —development of the Queen Bishop.

6 N—K5   . . . .

The alternative is 6 P—K3, P—K3; 7 BxP, B—QN5 (to restrain an eventual P—K4); 8 Castles, Castles; 9 Q—K2. Now Black can try to stop P—K4 or accept it as inevitable.

Thus: 9 . . . N—K5; 10 B—Q3! (an interesting Pawn sacrifice), BxN (if 10 . . . NxN; 11 PxN, BxP; 12 R—N1 and White regains the Pawn); 11 PxB!, NxQBP; 12 Q—B2, BxB; 13 QxB, N—Q4; 14 B—R3 with a magnificent development in return for the Pawn.

Or 9 . . . B—N5; 10 P—R3, BxN; 11 QxB, QN—Q2; 12 R—Q1 (not P—K4 at once because of . . . N—N3), P—K4!; 13 P—Q5! (if 13 PxP, NxP!), BxN!; 14 PxP!, P—K5!; 15 Q—B5, B—K4!; 16 PxN, Q—B2! and Black can just about hold his own.

96

(Position after 6 N—K5)

White intends to fianchetto his King Bishop. He will recover the gambit Pawn by capturing it with his King Knight.

6 ....   QN—Q2

Here 6 . . . P—K3 looks plausible, but after 7 P—B3! Black's Queen Bishop can run into trouble, for example 7 . . . B—QN5; 8 NxP/B4, Castles; 9 B—N5!, P—B4; 10 PxP, QxQch; 11 KxQ, BxP; 12 P—K4!, B—KN3; 13 N—K5. White will play NxB obtaining the positional advantage of two Bishops against Bishop and Knight.

7 NxP/B4	Q—B2	9 PxP	NxP
8 P—KN3!	P—K4	10 B—B4	N/B3—Q2
	11 B—N2	....	

97

(Position after 11 B—N2)

Black has developed freely and rapidly, but the pin on his King Knight promises to be troublesome.

| 11 .... | P—B3 | 13 Q—B1! | B—K3 |
| 12 Castles | R—Q1 | 14 N—K4! | .... |

The point is that after 14 ... BxN; 15 QxB, NxQ; 16 BxQ White has a very favorable endgame with his two Bishops against Bishop and Knight.

| 14 .... | B—QN5 | 15 P—R5! | .... |

White has a very strong position. If now 15 ... BxN; 16 QxB, BxP??; 17 Q—K6ch, K—B1; 18 KR—Q1! and White's pressure must be decisive. Or 15 ... Castles; 16 NxN, NxN; 17 N—B5 with powerful pressure.

(b) Semi-Slav: Classical Variation

1 P—Q4	P—Q4	3 N—KB3	N—B3
2 P—QB4	P—QB3	4 N—B3	P—K3
	5 P—K3	QN—Q2	

Against the "Stonewall" set-up of 5 ... N—K5; 6 B—Q3, P—KB4 White has the vigorous 7 P—KN4!!

| | 6 B—Q3 | B—Q3 | |

The conservative 6 ... B—K2 allows White to play 7 Castles, Castles; 8 P—QN3!, P—QN3; 9 B—N2 with a strong White initiative because his King Bishop's aggressive position contrasts favorably with the passive position of Black's King Bishop.

| 7 Castles | Castles | 8 P—K4! | .... |

98

(Position after 8 P—K4!)

White opens up the game advantageously, for if 8 . . . PxBP; 9 BxP, P—K4; 10 B—KN5! with a more aggressive development.

8	PxKP	9 NxP	NxN
10 BxN	N—B3		

Not 10 . . . P—K4?; 11 PxP, NxP; 12 NxN, BxN; 13 BxPch!, KxB; 14 Q—R5ch winning a Pawn.

           11 B—B2   ....

White has distinctly the freer game. Note that Black's Queen Bishop is still hemmed in.

(c) Semi-Slav: Meran Variation

1 P—Q4	P—Q4	5 P—K3	QN—Q2
2 P—QB4	P—QB3	6 B—Q3	PxP
3 N—KB3	N—B3	7 BxBP	P—QN4
4 N—B3	P—K3	8 B—Q3	....

99

(Position after 8 B—Q3)

Black can avoid the intricacies of the following play by continuing 8 ... B—N2; 9 P—K4, P—N5!; 10 N—QR4, P—B4; 11 P—K5, N—Q4 etc.

8	P—QR3	9 P—K4	....

After the colorless 9 Castles, P—B4; 10 P—QR4, P—N5; 11 N—K4, B—N2 Black has an easy game (generally true whenever he succeeds in developing the Queen Bishop).

9	P—B4!	10 P—K5	PxP!
11 NxNP!	NxP!		

If instead 11 ... PxN; 12 PxN, Q—N3; 13 PxP, BxP; 14 Castles, B—N2; 15 B—KB4, Castles KR and Black's King is somewhat exposed because of the missing King Knight Pawn.

12 NxN	PxN	13 Q—B3	....

100

(Position after 13 Q—B3)

To all appearances Black is in serious trouble, but he has ingenious resources.

| 13 .... | B—N5ch! | | 14 K—K2 | QR—N1 |

Calmly ignoring 15 N—B6, which he can answer with 15 . . . B—N2.

| 15 Q—N3 | Q—Q3! | | 17 RPxQ | B—Q3 |
| 16 N—B3 | QxQ | | 18 NxP | B—Q2 |

White has regained his Pawn, and the position is even. However, this variation is too complicated and dangerous for the average player.

(d) Semi-Slav: Anti-Meran Gambit

| 1 P—Q4 | P—Q4 | | 2 P—QB4 | P—QB3 |
| | | 3 N—KB3 | N—B3 | |

After 3 . . . P—K3 White can calmly protect the gambit Pawn with 4 P—K3—or he can go in for the complex alternative 4 N—B3!?, PxP; 5 P—K3, P—QN4; 6 P—QR4, B—N5; 7 B—Q2, P—QR4; 8 PxP, BxN; 9 BxB, PxP; 10 P—QN3!, B—N2!; 11 PxP, P—N5; 12 B—N2, N—KB3 and White's powerful center is more or less balanced by Black's bristling Queen-side passed Pawns.

| 4 N—B3 | P—K3 | | 5 B—N5!? | .... |

Avoiding the Meran Variation which could arise after 5 P—K3, QN—Q2; 6 B—Q3, PxP; 7 BxP, P—QN4 etc.

| 5 .... | PxP!? |

Leading to dangerous complications, whereas the sedate

alternative 5 . . . QN—Q2 would transpose into quieter lines like the Cambridge Springs Defense, Orthodox Defense, or Exchange Variation. After Black's last, 6 P—K3 is too slow because of 6 . . . P—N4. Therefore:

6 P—K4   P—N4   7 P—K5   P—KR3

This and Black's next move are forced.

8 B—R4   P—N4   9 NxKNP!   PxN

If 9 . . . N—Q4; 10 NxBP!, QxB; 11 NxR etc.

10 BxNP   QN—Q2

101

(Position after 10 . . . QN—Q2)

Though Black is temporarily a Pawn down and must lose back the extra piece, but he has excellent prospects. Thus, if 11 Q—B3, B—QN2; 12 B—K2, Q—N3!; 13 PxN, P—B4! with a splendid position.

11 P—KN3   Q—R4

A good alternative is 11 . . . B—QN2; 12 B—N2, Q—N3; 13 PxN, P—B4!; 14 PxP, BxP; 15 Castles, Castles.

12 PxN   P—N5   13 N—K4   B—QR3!

An exciting position in which both sides have weaknesses and attacking possibilities.

1 P—Q4	P—Q4	3 N—KB3	N—B3
2 P—QB4	P—QB3	4 P—K3	B—B4

Thus Black avoids the intricacies of the Meran Variation and develops his problem Bishop. But White manages to maintain the initiative.

5 B—Q3	BxB	7 N—B3	QN—Q2
6 QxB	P—K3	8 Castles	B—N5

Hoping—in vain—to stop P—K4. If instead 8 . . . B—Q3; 9 P—K4 with greater freedom of action for White.

$$9 \ B—Q2! \qquad \ldots .$$

102

(Position after 9 B—Q2!)

White has set a trap: if Black castles now, then 10 NxP! wins a Pawn.

9	B—R4	10 P—QN4!	B—B2

Not 10 . . . BxP; 11 NxP!, NxN; 12 PxN, BxB; 13 PxBP!, PxP; 14 NxB and White has a substantial positional advantage.

11 P—K4	PxBP	12 QxBP	. . . .

White has a noticeably freer game.

1 P—Q4	P—Q4
2 P—QB4	P—QB3
3 PxP	PxP

4 N—QB3	N—KB3
5 N—B3	N—B3
6 B—B4	....

103

(Position after 6 B—B4)

White's exchange at move 3 gives the variation its name. If now 6 . . . P—K3; 7 P—K3, B—K2 and Black's conservative development has the drawback of blocking his Queen Bishop's diagonal.

6	B—B4!

Black develops the problem Bishop, although he sees difficulties ahead.

7 P—K3	P—K3	8 Q—N3	B—QN5!

So that if 9 N—K5, Q—R4! counterattacking vigorously.

9 B—QN5	Castles!

Black is not afraid of 10 BxN, for then 10 . . . BxNch; 11 QxB, R—B1! is strong (12 Q—R3, RxB; 13 QxP, B—Q6!).

10 Castles	BxN	12 BxNP	BxR
11 BxN	BxNP	13 RxB	....

White must regain the Exchange, with a perfectly even position resulting.

Summary: Black's best practical chances seem to arise from the Meran and Anti-Meran lines in the Semi-Slav form. The deferred acceptance of the gambit is less suitable for Black because it leaves White with too much freedom of action.

ALBIN COUNTER GAMBIT

Like all gambits played by Black, this one must be viewed with suspicion. Black gives up a Pawn very early in the hope of gaining time for rapid development. White's cue is to develop quickly without attaching too much importance to the extra Pawn. The result is either that White keeps the extra Pawn and the initiative to boot; or else that he returns the Pawn and maintains powerful pressure.

1 P—Q4   P—Q4   2 P—QB4   P—K4?!

Rarely does Black have the opportunity to indulge in such violent play. This is good policy only against a definitely weaker opponent.

3 QPxP   P—Q5

The gambit is in operation. Black hopes that his advanced Queen Pawn will prove a stumbling block for White's development. More often than not, it becomes a target for White's pieces.

4 N—KB3   N—QB3   5 QN—Q2   . . . .

104

(Position after 5 QN—Q2)

In practically all variations White fianchettoes his King Bishop. This completes the mobilization of his King-side and gives the Bishop a powerful diagonal.

5 ....   B—K3

After 5 . . . P—B3; 6 PxP, NxP (or 6 . . . QxP) Black has inadequate compensation for the sacrificed Pawn.

On 5 . . . B—QN5 White has no objection to returning the extra Pawn, thus: 6 P—QR3!, BxNch; 7 QxB!, B—N5; 8 P—N4!, BxN; 9 KPxB, NxKP. For after 10 B—N2, Q—K2; 11 Castles, Castles; 12 P—B4 White has a marked positional advantage—two Bishops against two Knights.

Against 5 . . . B—KN5 White proceeds favorably with 6 P—KN3 etc.

6 P—KN3   Q—Q2   7 B—N2   R—Q1

Black can also castle at this point, but this leaves his King exposed to a withering attack based on the White King Bishop's long diagonal.

8 Castles   KN—K2   9 Q—R4   N—N3

Black hopes to win the advanced King Pawn—but this would cost him his Queen-side Pawns—thanks to the powerful action of White's pieces.

10 P—QR3!   B—K2   11 P—QN4   Castles

White continues 12 B—N2 with a very powerful position. Black cannot recover his Pawn, and his position has no appeal in other respects.

QUEEN'S GAMBIT ACCEPTED

In order to evade the difficult problems which confront the defender in the Queen's Gambit Declined, some players prefer to accept the gambit by answering 2 P—QB4 with 2 . . . PxP. This clears the long diagonal which extends out from Black's Queen Rook 1 square, and Black hopes to fianchetto his Queen Bishop to exploit this long diagonal.

Theoretically, this is an excellent notion—but there are drawbacks. Black's immediate surrender of the center gives White more space, quicker development, and the makings of a powerful Pawn center.

Black may try a different approach after 2 . . . PxP by developing his Queen Bishop to King Knight 5. Aggressive though this seems, White knows how to hit back hard. Thus the acceptance of the gambit involves Black in thorny problems.

(a) 4 . . . P—K3 Variation

| 1 P—Q4 | P—Q4 | 3 N—KB3 | N—KB3 |
| 2 P—QB4 | PxP | 4 P—K3 | P—K3 |

It is instructive to observe that it would be futile for Black to try to hold on to the gambit Pawn. Thus, if 4 . . . P—QN4; 5 P—QR4!, P—QB3; 6 P—QN3! No matter how Black plays, he loses back the Pawn and remains with a weakened Queen-side Pawn structure.

5 BxP   P—B4

An important counterthrust. By engaging the Queen Pawn at once, Black takes much of the sting out of an eventual P—K4 by White.

6 Castles   P—QR3   7 Q—K2   N—B3

105

(Position after 7 . . . N—B3)

White has two advantageous ways to proceed: 8 PxP! in order to fianchetto his Queen Bishop on a powerful diagonal; or 8 R—Q1! in order to operate on the center files with his Rooks.

Proceeding with inexorable logic, White can get a clear-cut positional advantage with 8 PxP!, BxP; 9 P—QR3!, P—QN4; 10 B—R2, B—N2; 11 P—QN4, B—K2; 12 B—N2, Castles; 13 QN—Q2! The point of White's play is clearly revealed in his last move: his Queen Knight can occupy the Queen Bishop 5 square. As for Black, his Queen Knight, being developed differently, cannot imitate this convincing maneuver.

There follows: 13 . . . Q—N3; 14 N—N3, KR—Q1; 15 QR—B1, QR—B1; 16 N—B5 with a distinctly superior position for White.

8 R—Q1   P—QN4

In order to answer 9 B—Q3 (or 9 B—N3) with 9 . . . P—B5!; 10 B—B2, N—QN5! and . . . NxB assuring Black the positional advantage of two Bishops against Bishop and Knight.

9 PxP	Q—B2	10 B—Q3	BxP

Not 10 . . . N—QN5; 11 P—QR4!, NxB; 12 QxN, P—N5; 13 P—B6! with a stranglehold on Black's game, as he cannot play 13 . . . QxBP?? because of 14 Q—Q8 mate.

	11 P—QR4!	P—N5

The alternative 11 . . . PxP; 12 RxP, N—QN5 is not appealing because of 13 B—N5ch!, B—Q2; 14 BxBch, NxB; 15 B—Q2 etc.

12 QN—Q2	Castles	12 N—N3	B—K2

White now plays 13 P—K4 followed by B—KN5 and QR—B1 leaving Black with a cramped, difficult game.

(b) 4 . . . B—N5 Variation

1 P—Q4	P—Q4	3 N—KB3	P—QR3
2 P—QB4	PxP	4 P—K3	B—N5

As we have already seen, it would be pointless for Black to play 4 . . . P—QN4 because of 5 P—QR4, P—QB3; 6 P—QN3! etc. Instead, he develops his Queen Bishop, pinning White's King Knight.

5 P—KR3	B—R4	6 BxP	P—K3
	7 Q—N3!	. . . .	

106

(Position after 7 Q—N3!)

Protecting the Queen Knight Pawn poses an awkward problem for Black, as neither 7 . . . Q—B1 nor 7 . . . R—R2 looks inviting.

7	BxN	9 B—K2	P—QB4
8 PxB	P—QN4	10 P—QR4	P—N5
	11 PxP	BxP	

White has two Bishops against Bishop and Knight, and he can make good use of the open King Knight file. In addition, Black's Queen-side Pawn structure has been weakened. The position definitely favors White.

MISCELLANEOUS DOUBLE QUEEN PAWN OPENINGS

There are openings in which White plays 1 P—Q4 and Black replies 1 . . . P—Q4, whereupon White deliberately avoids playing the Queen's Gambit. The result is an absence of tension in the central Pawn position. This lack of tension makes it easy for Black to achieve equality.

(a) Colle System

1 P—Q4	P—Q4	3 P—K3	P—B4
2 N—KB3	N—KB3	4 P—B3	. . . .

The characteristic move of this system. White's idea is to

support his Queen Bishop Pawn with a view to an eventual P—K4. This often gives him the initiative in the center. In turn such a preponderance, if met by indifferent moves, may lead to a powerful attack by White.

The alternative 4 P—QN3 has gone out of style because of the continuation 4 . . . P—K3; 5 B—N2, N—B3; 6 B—Q3, B—Q3; 7 Castles, Castles. Now if 8 QN—Q2, Q—K2!; 9 N—K5 (else Black frees himself at once with . . . P—K4), PxP; 10 PxP, B—R6 with an excellent game for Black. This applies also to 8 P—QR3, Q—B2 followed by . . . P—K4.

4 . . . .   QN—Q2!

An important finesse. After 4 . . . P—K3; 5 QN—Q2, N—B3; 6 B—Q3, B—Q3; 7 Castles, Castles; 8 PxP!, BxBP; 9 P—K4! White has the initiative in the center plus the Queen-side majority of Pawns. These advantages have led to some very impressive White victories with the Colle System.

107

(Position after 4 . . . QN—Q2!)

If now 5 QN—Q2, P—K3; 6 B—Q3, B—Q3; 7 Castles, Castles; 8 P—K4, BPxP!; 9 BPxP (not 9 NxP?, N—B4!), PxP; 10 NxP and White is left with the positional disadvantage of an isolated Queen Pawn.

5 QN—Q2   P—KN3

As the caption to Diagram 107 indicates, 5 . . . P—K3 is a perfectly suitable alternative. However, 5 . . . P—KN3 is even more promising, as it breaks the diagonal of White's

King Bishop and thereby crushes White's hopes of King-side attack.

Note that Black's 5 . . . P—KN3 is made possible by his previous move, which guards his Queen Bishop Pawn and gives him freedom of action.

6. B—Q3	B—N2	7 Castles	Castles

If now 8 P—K4, QPxP; 9 NxP, PxP; 10 NxP (not 10 PxP? leaving White with an isolated Queen Pawn), N—K4; 11 NxNch, BxN; 12 B—K2, B—Q2 and Black has more freedom of action.

We arrive at the same conclusion after 8 P—QN4, PxNP; 9 PxP, N—K1!; 10 B—N2, N—Q3; 11 Q—N3, N—N3; 12 P—QR4, B—B4!; 13 BxB, PxB! when White's remaining Bishop is hemmed in by its own Pawns.

(b) Stonewall Variation

1 P—Q4	P—Q4	3 B—Q3	P—B4
2 P—K3	N—KB3	4 P—QB3	. . . .

White intends to continue with P—KB4, establishing the Stonewall formation of his center Pawns. The force of this is best seen after the passive 4 . . . P—K3?; 5 P—KB4, QN—Q2; 6 N—B3, B—Q3; 7 QN—Q2, P—QN3; 8 N—K5, B—N2; 9 Q—B3, leaving White with a very powerful position in the center that often leads to an overwhelming attack.

4	N—B3

Black intends to proceed along different lines. He does not mind the possibility of 5 PxP, which gives him a tremendous Pawn center after 5 . . . P—K4. In any event, 5 PxP would be the negation of White's planned Stonewall set-up.

$$5 \text{ P—KB4} \qquad \text{B—N5!}$$

Immediately solving the problem of the troublesome Bishop.

6	N—B3	P—K3	9 P—QN3	PxP
7	QN—Q2	B—Q3	10 BPxP	QR—B1
8	P—KR3	B—R4	11 Castles	B—N3

Black has somewhat the better of it after 12 BxB, RPxB, as his remaining Bishop has more freedom of action than the White Bishop.

(c) 2 B—B4 Variation

$$1 \text{ P—Q4} \qquad \text{P—Q4} \qquad\qquad 2 \text{ B—B4} \qquad \ldots$$

This old-fashioned move is discredited nowadays for two reasons. In the first place, White gives Black the initiative in the center by permitting him to play . . . P—QB4. Secondly, White plays out his Queen Bishop before ascertaining what is the best square for that piece.

2	....	N—KB3	4 P—K3	N—B3
3	N—KB3	P—B4!	5 P—B3	Q—N3

Black is developing very comfortably.

6	Q—B1	B—B4	7 QN—Q2	P—K3

It is clear that White has frittered away the initiative. Black has a very promising game.

NIMZOINDIAN DEFENSE

In the "Indian" Defenses Black answers 1 P—Q4 with 1 . . . N—KB3. Momentarily, then, Black is trying to control the center by the Knight move (rather than the orthodox . . . P—Q4). Later on, Black may intensify this policy of controlling the center by using his pieces. On the other hand, he may resort to Pawn moves.

All this sounds inconsistent, but it really isn't. It puts a considerable burden on White, who must be prepared to contend with either policy on Black's part. Thus, in a psychological sense it may be said that 1 . . . N—KB3 is a subtle attempt on Black's part to dictate the course of the game.

As in the Queen's Gambit, the opening struggle in the Indian Defenses revolves about control of the center and freedom of the pieces. Whoever achieves the advantage in these respects will have the better game.

Now let us see how these theoretical concepts apply to the specific problems of the Nimzoindian Defense. Here are the opening moves:

1 P—Q4	N—KB3	2 P—QB4	P—K3
	3 N—QB3	. . . .	

Now White is on the point of playing 4 P—K4, with a Pawn center that would crush Black. Here is a crucial situation typical of the problems in this defense.

Of course, Black can solve the difficulty readily enough by playing 3 . . . P—Q4, getting his·fair share of the center by *transposing* into the . . . P—K3 defense of the Queen's Gambit Declined. But Black is intent on playing the Nimzoindian Defense. Therefore:

3 . . . .   B—N5

108

(Position after 3 . . . B—N5)

By pinning White's Queen Knight, Black makes it impossible for White to advance P—K4. Meanwhile Black conceals his intentions: He may play . . . P—Q4 or . . . P—Q3 later on— or perhaps not move the Queen Pawn altogether!

White has a great variety of replies at his disposal. Before we consider them, we will have to reflect on the possible forms that the struggle for the center may take.

For example, Black may play . . . P—Q4 later in order to stop White's extreme expansion in the center with P—K4.

Or Black may allow White to play P—K4, and proceed to build up a "counter-center" with . . . P—Q3 and . . . P—K4.

Another possibility is that Black may try . . . P—QB4 by way of a flank thrust at White's center.

But there are also other aspects to be considered. Black's 3 . . . B—N5 leads most of the time to an exchange of this Bishop for White's Queen Knight. In that case White has two Bishops against Bishop and Knight. This is a decided point in White's favor *if he also has a strong development.*

On the other hand, if Black develops rapidly and favorably (as generally happens in this defense), he can neutralize the theoretical advantage of the two Bishops.

This must be appraised in the light of still another problem. It often happens that when Black plays . . . BxN, White retakes with his Queen Knight Pawn. This supports his Queen Pawn and is likely to give him the makings of a powerful Pawn center.

On the other hand, Black reasons that the doubled Queen

Bishop Pawn is a weakness, and he may elect to train his guns on the Pawn at White's Queen Bishop 4 square.

Who is right? It all depends on how the game continues. What we have here is a struggle of extreme tension, in which each player attempts to cash his own potential advantages and nullify those of his opponent. In the detailed analysis that follows, you will repeatedly observe the clash between the rival conceptions.

These comments explain the widespread popularity of the Nimzoindian Defense. It offers great rewards to an enterprising and inventive player.

(a) 4 Q—B2 Variation with 4 . . . P—Q4

1 P—Q4	N—KB3	3 N—QB3	B—N5
2 P—QB4	P—K3	4 Q—B2	. . . .

Renewing the struggle for the center. White is on the point of playing P—K4.

$$4 \ldots \ldots \qquad P—Q4$$

109

(Position after 4 . . . P—Q4)

By advancing his Queen Pawn to Queen 4 Black has adopted the simplest way to maintain a foothold in the center.

Now 5 P—QR3 looks obvious, in order to get rid of the pin, but after 5 . . . BxNch; 6 QxB, N—K5; 7 Q—B2, extremely wild play may result:

7 ... P—QB4; 8 QPxP, N—QB3; 9 N—B3, Q—R4ch;
10 N—Q2, N—Q5; 11 Q—Q3, P—K4!?; 12 P—QN4,
Q—R5; 13 R—R2!

Or 7 ... N—QB3; 8 P—K3, P—K4!?; 9 BPxP, QxP;
10 B—B4, Q—R4ch; 11 P—QN4, NxNP; 12 QxN, N—B7
dbl ch; 13 K—K2, Q—K8ch; 14 K—B3, NxR; 15 B—N2.

In either case we have wild complications which the average player does well to steer clear of.

5 PxP ....

110

(Position after 5 PxP)

*Again Black must make a choice: to
command the center with pieces (5
... QxP) or the Queen Pawn (5 ...
PxP).*

The simplest method of recapture is 5 ... PxP. If then
6 B—N5, P—KR3; 7 BxN, QxB; 8 P—QR3, BxNch; 9
QxB, P—B3; 10 P—K3, Castles; 11 N—B3, B—B4 and
Black stands well.

Note that after 6 B—N5, P—KR3; 7 B—R4 allows Black
to counterattack vigorously with 7 ... P—B4!, for example
8 PxP, N—B3; 9 Castles, P—KN4!; 10 B—N3, Q—R4 etc.

5 .... QxP 6 N—B3 P—B4

Operating against White's Pawn center.

7 B—Q2 BxN

In order to maintain the centralized position of his Queen.

| 8 BxB | PxP | 9 NxP | P—K4 |

A valuable freeing move. If now 10 N—B5, BxN; 11 QxB, N—B3; 12 P—K3, Castles; 13 B—K2, Q—K5! with equality.

| 10 N—B3 | N—B3 | 12 B—K2 | B—N5 |
| 11 P—K3 | Castles | 13 P—KR3 | .... |

Equal game. White has the two Bishops, but Black has freedom of action, for example 13 . . . B—R4; 14 Castles KR, KR—Q1; 15 P—R3, B—N3; 16 Q—B1, N—K5 etc.

(b) 4 Q—B2 Variation with 4 . . . N—B3

| 1 P—Q4 | N—KB3 | 3 N—QB3 | B—N5 |
| 2 P—QB4 | P—K3 | 4 Q—B2 | N—B3 |

Gaining time by attacking White's Queen Pawn and preparing to build up a center with . . . P—Q3 and . . . P—K4.

| 5 N—B3 | P—Q3 |

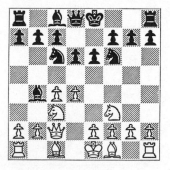

111

(Position after 5 . . . P—Q3)

Black is prepared to concede the two Bishops to White, as the forthcoming . . . P—K4 will maintain the balance of power in the center.

If now 6 P—QR3, BxNch; 7 QxB White has the two Bishops and Black must play carefully to avoid a constricted position. 7 . . . P—QR4! prevents too much White expansion (by 8 P—QN4). Then, after 8 P—QN3, Castles; 9 B—N2 Black plays for . . . P—K4 with 9 . . . R—K1!; 10 R—Q1, Q—K2! etc.

| 6 B—Q2 | P—K4 | 8 BxB | Q—K2 |
| 7 P—QR3 | BxN | 9 PxP | .... |

Loosening up the position so that his Queen Bishop will have more scope.

| 9 .... | PxP | 10 P—K3 | P—QR4! |

Again preventing White from expanding unduly with P—QN4 (threatening P—N5).

| | 11 P—R3! | .... | |

Preventing the development of Black's Queen Bishop via . . . B—N5. But Black has a resourceful continuation.

| 11 .... | Castles | 12 B—K2 | P—KN3! |

Black maintains equality by preparing . . . B—B4. After 13 P—QN3, B—B4; 14 Q—N2, KR—K1; 15 Castles, N—K5 the position is approximately even.

(c) 4 Q—B2 Variation with 4 . . . P—B4

| 1 P—Q4 | N—KB3 | 3 N—QB3 | B—N5 |
| 2 P—QB4 | P—K3 | 4 Q—B2 | P—B4 |

This flank thrust is intended to demolish White's center by removing White's Queen Pawn. White generally gets pressure on the opened Queen file and on the opened long diagonal extending from his Queen Rook 1 to King Rook 8. However, Black can equalize by getting good play for his pieces in the center.

5 PxP   ....

112

(Position after 5 PxP)

Black can hold his own with 5 . . . BxP; 6 N—B3, N—B3; 7 B—N5, B—K2 followed by . . . P—Q3. But this leads to a cramped position which is not to everyone's taste.

5 ....   Castles

And now the pinning move 6 B—N5 looks good. However, Black counterattacks effectively with 6 . . . N—R3!; 7 P—QR3, BxNch; 8 QxB, NxP. White has the two Bishops, but Black has a good grip on the center, for example 9 Q—B2 (to avoid . . . N/B4—K5), P—QR4!; 10 P—B3, P—R5; 11 R—Q1, N—N6; 12 P—K4, Q—R4ch; 13 B—Q2, NxB; 14 QxN, P—Q4 and Black has at least equality.

6 N—B3   N—R3!

Here too the Knight arrives rapidly at an influential post for controlling the center. If now 7 P—QR3, BxNch! 8 QxB, NxP; 9 P—QN4, N/B4—K5 and Black's commanding centralized position makes up for White's two Bishops.

| 7 B—Q2 | NxP | 8 P—QR3 | BxN |
| | 9 BxB | N/B4—K5 | |

As in the previous note, Black has equality, thanks to the fine position of his centralized Knight.

(d) 4 P—K3 Variation

| 1 P—Q4 | N—KB3 | 3 N—QB3 | B—N5 |
| 2 P—QB4 | P—K3 | 4 P—K3 | .... |

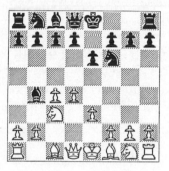

113

(Position after 4 P—K3)

White's last move is stronger than it looks. He prepares the development of his King Bishop and is ready to benefit by any advantages that may accrue from his having the Bishop-pair after . . . BxN.

If now 4 . . . Castles, the play may very likely transpose into one of the variations shown below. An independent possibility is 5 KN—K2, P—Q4; 6 P—QR3, B—K2; 7 PxP, PxP; 8 P—KN3 (much more promising than 8 N—N3, P—B4! and if 9 PxP, BxP; 10 P—N4, P—Q5!), QN—Q2; 9 B—N2, N—N3; 10 Q—Q3, P—QR4; 11 P—QR4, P—B3; 12 Castles, QN—Q2; 13 P—B3; with the idea of forming a powerful Pawn center with P—K4.

Against 4 . . . P—QN3 White can also proceed with 5 KN—K2 and if 5 . . . B—R3; 6 P—QR3, B—K2; 7 N—B4, P—Q4; 8 PxP, BxB; 9 KxB, PxP; 10 P—KN4! with a strong initiative.

Another way is 4 . . . P—QN3; 5 KN—K2, B—N2; 6 P—QR3, BxNch; 7 NxB, Castles; 8 B—Q3!, P—B4 (not 8 . . . BxP; 9 KR—N1, B—N2; 10 P—K4 followed by P—K5 with a withering attack); 9 P—Q5! cramping Black's game considerably. If then 9 . . . PxP; 10 PxP, NxP?; 11 NxN, BxN; 12 Q—R5—or 10 . . . BxP?; 11 NxB, NxN; 12 B—K4 and White wins in either event.

4	P—Q4	5 B—Q3	Castles

If White now continues 6 N—B3, P—B4; 7 Castles, N—B3; 8 P—QR3, Black's simplest course is 8 . . . BxN; 9 PxB, P—QN3 with good prospects for Black despite White's two Bishops.

Or Black may try (after 8 P—QR3) 8 . . . QPxP; 9 BxBP, PxP; 10 PxP, B—K2. Then after 11 Q—Q3, P—QN3; 12 B—R2, B—N2; 13 B—N1, P—N3 White has a freer game and attacking chances, while Black has pressure on White's isolated Queen Pawn.

6 P—QR3	BxNch	7 PxB	....

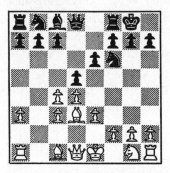

114

(Position after 7 PxB)

White's sturdy Pawn center and his possession of two Bishops give him many powerful attacking chances.

Black must handle the defense with great care. Thus, after

7 . . . P—B4; 8 BPxP!, KPxP; 9 N—K2, P—QN3; 10 Castles, B—R3; 11 BxB, NxB; 12 Q—Q3 White has the makings of a powerful attack despite the disappearance of his attacking Bishop. The sequel might be 12 . . . P—B5; 13 Q—B2, N—N1; 14 P—B3!, R—K1; 15 N—N3, N—B3; 16 Q—B2, Q—Q2; 17 B—N2, R—K3; 18 QR—K1, QR—K1 (Black strives in vain to prevent P—K4); 19 R—K2, P—N3; 20 KR—K1, N—QR4; 21 P—K4, Q—N2; 22 P—K5 followed by P—B4 with a formidable "Pawn-roller."

7	PxP!	10 Castles	Q—B2!
8 BxBP	P—B4	11 B—Q3	P—K4
9 N—B3	N—B3	12 Q—B2	....

An intensely interesting position. Black has freed himself admirably, but White hopes to open up the position and get his center Pawns moving so that he can demonstrate the power of his Bishops.

A possibility is 12 . . . R—Q1; 13 R—K1, B—N5; 14 NxP, NxN; 15 PxN, QxP; 16 P—B3, B—K3; 17 R—N1, P—B5; 18 B—B1, N—Q4!; 19 B—Q2, Q—B2.

A wilder line of play is 12 . . . R—K1 (threatens . . . P—K5); 13 P—K4, KPxP; 14 PxP, B—N5!; 15 P—K5, BxN; 16 PxN, NxQP; 17 BxPch, K—R1; 18 PxPch, KxP; 19 B—N2!; QR—Q1!; 20 PxB, R—KR1!; 21 K—R1, RxB.

In both cases Black holds his own because the free play of his pieces compensates for White's Bishop-pair. This is often the verdict on Nimzoindian variations.

(e) 4 P—QR3 Variation

| 1 P—Q4 | N—KB3 | 3 N—QB3 | B—N5 |
| 2 P—QB4 | P—K3 | 4 P—QR3 | .... |

This leads to a very difficult game for both sides. After the following exchange White hopes to get a good attack, based on his two Bishops and his powerful-looking Pawn center. Black hopes for a close position where his Knights can maneuver skillfully; he also has prospects of turning White's Pawn at Queen Bishop 4 into a target.

4 ....　　　　BxNch　　　　5 PxB　　　　....

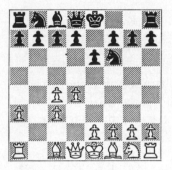

115

(Position after 5 PxB)

Note that White's Pawn at Queen Bishop 4 can no longer be protected by Pawns, and must be protected by pieces. Hence this Pawn is weak, and Black will try to train his guns on it.

5 ....　　　　P—B4!

This "fixes" White's theoretically weak Pawn at White's Queen Bishop 4. In addition, Black exerts pressure on White's Pawn center.

6 P—K3　　　　P—QN3

Black's Bishop will go to Queen Knight 2 (later to Queen Rook 3, to press against the weak Pawn).

On the other hand, playing for an early . . . P—K4 is doubtful policy, as it often allows White to open the King Bishop file with impressive effect, for example 6 . . . N—B3; 7 B—Q3, P—K4; 8 N—K2, P—Q3; 9 Castles, Q—K2; 10 P—K4!, N—Q2; 11 P—B4, P—QN3; 12 N—N3, P—N3;

13 BPxP, QPxP; 14 P—Q5, N—QR4; 15 R—R2!, N—N2;
16 QR—KB2, N—Q3; 17 B—R6 with considerable positional advantage for White.

| 7 B—Q3 | B—N2 | 9 N—K2 | Castles |
| 8 P—B3 | N—B3 | 10 P—K4 | N—K1! |

A star move. To allow the pinning maneuver B—N5 would
be fatal to Black's freedom of action. The retreat of the
Knight also prepares for the blockading move . . . P—B4.

| 11 B—K3 | P—Q3 | 12 Castles | N—R4! |

116

(Position after 12 . . . N—R4!)

Black begins the attack on the Queen Bishop Pawn.

*Black has the initiative, as Black's threats against the
Queen Bishop Pawn outweigh White's attacking possibilities
on the other wing. For example: 13 N—N3, Q—Q2; 14 P—
B4, P—B4; 15 Q—K2 (if 15 QPxP, QPxP; 16 PxP, R—
Q1!), P—N3!; 16 KR—Q1, N—N2; 17 R—R2, Q—R5!;
18 B—B1, QR—B1! (note the mounting pressure on White's
Queen Bishop Pawn); 19 Q—QB2, QxQ; 20 RxQ, B—R3!
and Black wins the weak Queen Bishop Pawn.*

QUEEN'S INDIAN DEFENSE

In this defense Black fianchettoes his Queen Bishop very early, with a view to commanding the long diagonal, particularly his King 5 square. White does best to fianchetto his King Bishop, thus carrying on a long-range duel for control of the diagonal.

This duel often centers about a specific problem: White wants to enforce P—K4, Black wants to prevent this move. If White gets in P—K4, he will have an advantage in space, which explains the critical nature of the struggle. Bear in mind, though, that since White plays an early N—KB3 (instead of N—QB3 as in the Nimzoindian Defense), it will not be easy for him to enforce P—K4.

On the whole, White gets a freer game than Black in this opening. White's goal is to secure the initiative; Black's goal is to maintain an adequate defense.

(a) 5 ... B—K2 Variation

1 P—Q4	N—KB3	4 P—KN3	B—N2
2 P—QB4	P—K3	5 B—N2	B—K2
3 N—KB3	P—QN3	6 Castles	Castles
	7 N—B3	. . . .	

Black can now get a firm foothold in the center with 7 . . . P—Q4 at the cost of condemning his Queen Bishop to inactivity after 8 N—K5!

7	N—K5	8 Q—B2	NxN

White's next move is more or less forced, as 9 PxN would give him a doubled Queen Bishop Pawn with no tangible compensation.

9 QxN   ....

117

(Position after 9 QxN)

Black has a double goal: to retain control of his King 5 square, and also to form a center of his own by ... P—Q3 and ... P—K4.

White has good chances of getting the initiative: if for example 9 ... P—KB4; 10 P—Q5!, PxP; 11 N—K1 *with lasting pressure on Black's game.*

Another possibility from Diagram 40 is 9 ... B—K5; 10 B—B4!, P—Q3; 11 Q—K3!, B—N2; 12 KR—Q1, N—Q2; 13 P—QN4, N—B3; 14 P—QR4, P—QR4; 15 P—N5 *and White has considerably more freedom of action.*

(b) 5 ... B—N5ch Variation

1 P—Q4	N—KB3	3 N—KB3	P—QN3
2 P—QB4	P—K3	4 P—KN3	B—N2
	5 B—N2	....	

118

(Position after 5 B—N2)

Black decides on a simplifying exchange, which, however, still leaves him with difficult problems to solve.

| 5 .... | B—N5ch | 6 B—Q2 | BxBch |

The obvious reply is now 7 QNxB. But White's Queen Knight will be more aggressively posted at Queen Bishop 3 than at Queen 2. This explains White's next move:

| 7 QxB! | Castles | 8 N—B3 | P—Q3 |

After this White will be able to play P—K4, but if instead 8 . . . N—K5; 9 Q—B2!, NxN; 10 N—N5! winning the Exchange because of the mate threat.

| 9 Q—B2 | Q—K2 | 10 Castles KR | P—B4 |

Black must forestall P—K4, which would permit White to answer a later . . . P—B4 with P—Q5, seriously constricting Black's game.

| 11 QR—Q1 | PxP | 12 NxP | BxB |

After 13 KxB White is on the way to playing P—K4, which will give him a much greater command of the board. White has an unmistakable initiative.

KING'S INDIAN DEFENSE

This is generally considered the most complex and most interesting of all the Indian Defenses. As in other "Indian" lines, Black avoids answering 1 P—Q4 with 1 . . . P—Q4. Instead, he plays 1 . . . N—KB3 and continues with . . . P—KN3 and . . . B—N2.

Of course, he cannot wholly neglect the center. He almost invariably plays . . . P—Q3 followed in due course by . . . P—K4. After that, he has several possibilities. One is to play . . . KPxQP, opening up the long diagonal for his fianchettoed Bishop. This has the customary drawback of freeing White's position as well.

Or Black may stand pat after . . . P—K4, giving White the opportunity to push by with P—Q5, which leads to a rather locked position in which the advantage generally goes to the player who can first advance his King Bishop Pawn two squares.

Theoretically, White ought to have the advantage because his position is freer. But Black's position is solid and full of resource; a tenacious player can accomplish miracles with this defense.

(a) 3 P—KN3 Variation with . . . P—Q3

| 1 P—Q4 | N—KB3 | 3 P—KN3 | B—N2 |
| 2 P—QB4 | P—KN3 | 4 B—N2 | Castles |

Experience has shown that fianchettoing is an effective way to develop White's King Bishop.

| 5 P—K4 | P—Q3 | 6 N—K2 | . . . . |

All in all this is preferable to N—KB3. At King 2 this Knight does not stand in the way of P—B4.

| 6 .... | P—K4 | 7 QN—B3 | .... |

Also possible is 7 P—Q5, which on the whole seems to give White preferable chances. For he can strive to gain further terrain with P—B4, as well as P—QN4 followed by P—QB5. A likely sequel is 7 . . . P—QR4; 8 Castles, QN—Q2; 9 QN—B3, N—B4; 10 P—KR3, N—K1; 11 B—K3, P—B4; 12 PxP, PxP; 13 P—B4, and White's game is more promising.

| 7 .... | QN—Q2 | 8 Castles | P—B3 |

In order to be able to play . . . Q—B2 or . . . Q—N3. In some cases the move prepares for an eventual . . . P—Q4, which is, however, too ambitious a project.

| | 9 P—KR3! | .... |

White wants to play B—K3, but first he rules out the annoying . . . N—N5.

| 9 .... | PxP | 10 NxP | .... |

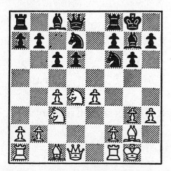

119

(Position after 10 NxP)

Black has obtained maneuvering freedom for his Knights and King Bishop. However, his weakened Queen Pawn is readily subject to pressure.

Black has numerous possibilities here, but White maintains the upper hand with accurate play. Thus, if 10 . . . R—K1; 11 B—K3, N—N3; 12 P—N3, P—Q4?; 13 KPxP, PxP; 14 P—B5, QN—Q2; 15 KN—N5!, Q—R4; 16 P—R3!, N—K5?!; 17 P—QN4, NxN; 18 NxN, Q—Q1; 19 NxP!, BxR; 20 QxB and White has an overwhelming game in return for the sacrifice of the Exchange.

Another possibility is 10 . . . R—K1; 11 B—K3 (also good is 11 R—K1, N—B4; 12 B—B4 with pressure on the Queen Pawn), N—B4; 12 Q—B2, P—QR4; 13 QR—Q1 (threatens 14 NxP!, PxN; 15 BxN), Q—K2; 14 KR—K1 and White has a fine game. (Note the trap 14 . . . KNxP?; 15 NxN, NxN; 16 BxN, QxB; 17 B—Q2! and White wins!)

The superior development of White's pieces assures him the better game with careful play.

(b) 3 . . . P—KN3 Variation with . . . P—Q4

1 P—Q4	N—KB3	3 P—KN3	B—N2
2 P—QB4	P—KN3	4 B—N2	P—Q4
	5 PxP	NxP	

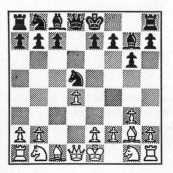

120

(Position after 5 . . . NxP)

White plans to get a powerful center Pawn position. Black hopes to prove that White's plans are too ambitious.

6 P—K4   N—N3

Though 6 . . . N—N5 is playable, it involves tactical finesses, for example 7 Q—R4ch, QN—B3; 8 P—Q5, P—QN4! (even 8 . . . Castles! is possible, for if 9 PxN, N—Q6ch and Black regains the piece); 9 QxNP (or 9 Q—N3?, N—Q5!), N—B7ch; 10 K—Q1, B—Q2 and White cannot play 11 KxN?? N—Q5ch nor 11 PxN??, BxP dis ch. And after 6 . . . N—N5; 7 P—Q5, P—QB3; 8 N—K2 (8 P—QR3 is best answered by 8 . . . Q—R4!), PxP; 9 PxP, B—KB4; 10 Q—R4ch, QN—B3!; 11 QN—B3! (not 11 PxN??, N—B7ch; 12 K—B1, Q—Q8 mate), B—B7! or . . . P—QN4! and Black can hold his own in the coming complications.

7 N—K2   . . . .

Immediate measures against White's center are futile, for example 7 . . . P—K4; 8 P—Q5, P—QB3; 9 QN—B3, PxP; 10 PxP and White's passed Pawn is a power for the endgame.

7 . . . .   Castles   8 Castles   . . . .

121

(Position after 8 Castles)

Black cannot make any headway against White's powerful center. For example 8 . . . P—QB4; 9 P—Q5 and Black's Knights have no prospects.

8	N—B3	12 PxP	N—B5
9 P—Q5	N—N1	13 R—K1	R—K1
10 KN—B3!	P—QB3	14 N—R3!	N—Q3
11 P—QR4!	PxP	15 QN—N5!	. . . .

White's pressure is stifling. But the avoidance of this line (with 6 . . . N—N5) requires first-class tactical abilities.

(c) B—K2 Variation

1 P—Q4	N—KB3	4 P—K4	P—Q3
2 P—QB4	P—KN3	5 B—K2	Castles
3 N—QB3	B—N2	6 P—B4	. . . .

A plausible-looking alternative is 6 B—N5, but Black can take advantage of the absence of White's Queen Bishop from the Queen-side in this fashion: 6 . . . P—B4!; 7 P—Q5, P—K3; 8 N—B3, PxP; 9 BPxP, P—KR3; 10 B—KB4, P—QN4!; 11 BxNP, NxKP!; 12 NxN, Q—R4ch; 13 Q—Q2, QxB; 14 NxQP, QxP; 15 QxQ, BxQ; 16 QR—N1, B—B6ch; 17 K—Q1, B—R3; 18 BxP, R—Q1; 19 B—B4, B—R4! and the threat of . . . B—B2 enables Black to regain his Pawn with a superior position, thanks to his two Bishops.

> 6 . . . .   P—K4

Black does not fear 7 PxP, PxP; 8 NxP which he can answer with 8 . . . NxP!

> 7 Castles   N—B3!

The old move was 7 . . . QN—Q2, which allowed Black to equalize after 8 R—K1, P—B3; 9 B—B1, R—K1; 10 P—QN3, PxP!; 11 NxP, P—Q4! or 10 R—N1, PxP; 11 NxP, P—Q4!

However, on 7 . . . QN—Q2 White maintains the initiative with 8 P—Q5, N—B4; 9 Q—B2, P—QR4; 10 N—K1!, KN—Q2; 11 B—K3, P—B4; 12 PxP, PxP; 13 P—B4, P—K5; 14 Q—Q2, N—B3; 15 N—B2. White will eventually break through with P—KN4. Meanwhile he commands his vital Queen 4 square and more than adequately blockades Black's passed Pawn.

8 P—Q5	N—K2		10 B—K3	P—KB4
9 N—K1	N—Q2!		11 P—B3	P—B5
	12 B—B2	P—KN4		

122

(Position after 12 . . . P—KN4)

A very exciting position. White attacks on the Queen-side, intending to open lines there with P—B5. Black attacks on the King-side, intending to open lines there with . . . P—N5.

13 N—Q3   N—KB3

Another way is . . . R—B3 followed by . . . R—N3 intending . . . P—N5.

| 14 P—B5 | N—N3 | | 16 PxP | PxP |
| 15 R—B1 | R—B2 | | 17 N—QN5 | P—N5 |

Both sides have carried out their plans according to schedule, and a fierce fight is in progress.

(d) Saemisch Variation

1 P—Q4	N—KB3		4 P—K4	P—Q3
2 P—QB4	P—KN3		5 P—B3	Castles
3 N—QB3	B—N2		6 B—K3	P—K4
	7 P—Q5		....	

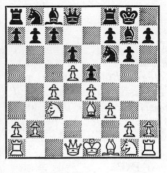

123

(Position after 7 P—Q5)

White's solid 5th move is the key to this variation. He delays somewhat the development of his King-side while he prepares to castle on the other wing and begin an attack with P—KN4 and P—KR4 etc.

7	P—B4		10 PxP	PxP
8 Q—Q2	N—R4		11 B—Q3	P—QR3
9 Castles	P—B4		12 KN—K2	P—N4?!

Black offers a Pawn in order to open attacking lines against the hostile King. But White is more interested in furthering his own attack.

13 QR—N1	PxP		14 B—N1!	....

Played in order to lend greater strength to White's coming P—KN4. *White's attack on the open file should then win for him.*

(e) Four Pawns' Variation

1 P—Q4	N—KB3		3 N—QB3	B—N2
2 P—QB4	P—KN3		4 P—K4	P—Q3
	5 P—B4		....	

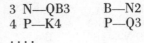

(Position after 5 P—B4)

White's last move is very aggressive and may leave Black with a very cramped game. On the other hand, the slightest inexactitude on White's part may grant Black a powerful counterattack.

5	P—B4	6 PxP!	....

Best. After 6 P—Q5, Castles; 7 N—B3, P—K4! Black's game is quite solid (8 PxP, PxP; 9 NxP, NxP!).

After the text, 6 . . . PxP; 7 QxQch, KxQ; 8 P—K5 gives Black a poor game.

6	Q—R4

Threatens . . . NxP.

7 B—Q3	QxBP	8 Q—K2	N—B3

White now continues 9 N—B3 followed by B—K3, after which his more harmonious development should tell in his favor.

Summary: On the whole, White's best chance of obtaining a solid positional advantage stems from the early fianchetto of his King Bishop—Variation (*a*).

GRUENFELD DEFENSE

In this Indian Defense, Black combines the fianchetto of his King Bishop with . . . P—Q4. As a rule, Black's Queen Pawn disappears quickly, allowing White to set up an impressive Pawn center.

To make up for White's advantage in this respect, Black must concentrate on agile maneuvers with his pieces. In some cases, he can hit back at White's center with . . . P—QB4. At all times Black must be prepared to put his King Bishop to good use on the long diagonal.

(a) Exchange Variation

1 P—Q4	N—KB3		3 N—QB3	P—Q4
2 P—QB4	P—KN3		4 PxP	. . . .

White sets out at once to build up a Pawn center. After the quiet alternative 4 P—K3, B—N2; 5 N—B3, Castles; 6 Q—N3, P—K3, 7 B—Q2, P—N3 Black fianchettoes his other Bishop with a good game.

4	NxP		5 P—K4	NxN
6 PxN	P—QB4!			

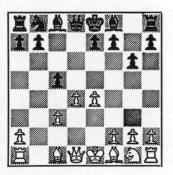

125

(Position after 6 . . . P—QB4!)

Black loses no time in hitting at White's powerful Pawn center. Black will immediately intensify the pressure with . . . B—N2.

| 7 B—QB4 | B—N2 | | 8 N—K2! | .... |

The more aggressive-looking N—B3 allows a future pin by . . . B—N5.

| 8 .... | Castles | | 10 PxP | N—B3 |
| 9 Castles | PxP | | 11 B—K3 | .... |

126

(Position after 11 B—K3)

A crucial position, as Black must now be prepared to demonstrate the effectiveness of his pressure on the center Pawns.

| 12 .... | N—R4! | | 13 B—Q3 | N—B3! |

Thus Black establishes equality. White must guard his Queen Pawn, and if 14 B—QB4, N—R4 etc. threatens to repeat moves indefinitely. If 14 B—B2, P—N3 intending 15 . . . N—N5; 16 B—N3, B—QR3 with an excellent game for Black.

(b) 5 Q—N3 Variation

1 P—Q4	N—KB3		3 N—QB3	P—Q4
2 P—QB4	P—KN3		4 N—B3	B—N2
	5 Q—N3		....	

127

(Position after 5 Q—N3)

White insists on clearing up the position in the center. As 5 . . . P—K3 or 5 . . . P—B3 would be rather passive, Black gives up the center in the hope of getting active play for his pieces.

| 5 .... | PxP | 6 QxBP | Castles |

As in the previous variation, White now creates an imposing Pawn center.

| | 7 P—K4 | B—N5 |

Black attacks the Knight which guards White's Queen Pawn.

| 8 B—K3 | KN—Q2 | 9 Q—N3 | N—N3 |

128

(Position after 9 . . . N—N3)

White's Queen Pawn is under pressure, now that the Black King Knight has unmasked the diagonal of Black's King Bishop. However, White has ample resources.

| 10 R—Q1 | N—B3 | 12 B—K2 | NxNch |
| 11 P—Q5 | N—K4 | 13 PxN | B—R6 |

White has considerably more maneuvering space for his pieces, and after 14 KR—N1, Q—B1; 15 P—B4!, B—Q2; 16 P—B5! he has a formidable attack.

(c) 4 B—B4 Variation

1 P—Q4	N—KB3	3 N—QB3	P—Q4
2 P—QB4	P—KN3	4 B—B4	B—N2
	5 P—K3	Castles!	

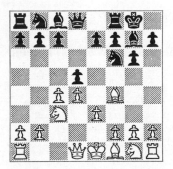

129

(Position after 5 . . . Castles!)

Black's last move amounts to a gambit, as White can now win a Pawn. However, Black's threats assure him adequate compensation.

After 6 PxP, NxP; 7 NxN, QxN; 8 BxP White has won a Pawn. However, Black gets a very strong game with 8 . . . N—R3! for example 9 B—N3, B—B4 (threatens . . . N—N5); 10 P—QR3, QR—B1 with a view to . . . R—B7. Also possible is 8 . . . N—R3!; 9 BxN, PxB when White's most prudent course is 10 N—B3 allowing Black to regain the Pawn with 10 . . . Q—N2. If instead 10 Q—B3, Q—QN4!! when 11 QxR will not do because of 11 . . . QxP; 12 R—Q1, Q—B6ch; 13 R—Q2, B—N5! and wins.

| 6 R—B1 | P—B4! | | 7 QPxP | B—K3! |

Black stands well despite the Pawn minus, for example 8 PxP, NxP; 9 NxN, BxN; 10 P—QN3, Q—R4ch; 11 Q—Q2, QxQch; 12 KxQ, R—Q1 etc.

Summary: White should rely on his Pawn center, while Black should strive for utmost mobility. Variation (*b*) favors White, while the other two lines are satisfactory for Black.

BLUMENFELD COUNTER GAMBIT

As we have seen earlier, counter gambits, being attempts to wrest the initiative out of White's hands, have slight chance to succeed. This reasoning applies to the Blumenfeld line.

| 1 P—Q4 | N—KB3 | | 3 N—KB3 | P—B4 |
| 2 P—QB4 | P—K3 | | 4 P—Q5 | P—QN4?! |

Risky—and unnecessary as well, as the simple 4 . . . PxP transposes into the Benoni line described on page 163. Black hopes for the speculative continuation 5 QPxP, BPxP; 6 PxP, P—Q4 which gives him a strong center and open lines for his pieces in return for a relatively unimportant wing Pawn.

| 5 B—N5! | KPxP |

Another way, just as disadvantageous, is 5 . . . Q—R4ch; 6 Q—Q2, QxQch; 7 QNxQ, KPxP; 8 BxN, PxB; 9 PxQP, B—QN2; 10 P—K4, P—QR3; 11 N—R4 with considerable positional advantage for White.

6 PxQP	P—KR3		9 P—K4	P—R3
7 BxN	QxB		10 P—QR4	P—N5
8 Q—B2	P—Q3		11 P—R3!	....

With his last move, White has hemmed in Black's Queen Bishop. After 11 . . . B—K2; 12 QN—Q2, Castles; 13 B—K2, N—Q2; 14 N—B4 White has considerably greater freedom of action. Black's two Bishops can accomplish little.

BUDAPEST DEFENSE

This is also a counter gambit, but it has more positional justification than most defenses of its kind. If White clings slavishly to the gained material, he often gets into trouble. On the other hand, if he develops systematically, he is likely to get the better game. A too rapid advance, however, should be shunned, as it may enable Black to counterattack successfully.

(a) 4 B—B4 Variation

1 P—Q4   N—KB3   2 P—QB4   P—K4

This is the counter gambit.

3 PxP   . . . .

130

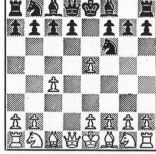

(Position after 3 PxP)

If Black tries 3 . . . N—K5, White continues with simple development: 4 N—KB3, N—QB3; 5 QN—Q2, N—B4; 6 P—KN3, P—Q3; 7 PxP, QxP; 8 B—N2, B—B4; 9 P—QR3, P—QR4; 10 Castles, Castles; 11 P—QN4! returning the Pawn for a winning attack.

3 . . . .   N—N5

And now 4 P—B4? would be quite bad: 4 . . . B—B4; 5 N—R3, P—KB3 with an overwhelming game for Black.

4 B—B4   N—QB3   5 N—KB3   B—N5ch

131

(Position after 5 . . . B—N5ch)

If now 6 N—B3, Q—K2; 7 Q—Q5, BxNch; 8 PxB, P—B3! and White's extra Pawn, being doubled and isolated, is not worth much.

6 QN—Q2   Q—K2   7 P—QR3   KNxKP

If now 8 PxB???, N—Q6 mate.

8 NxN   NxN   10 QxB   P—Q3
9 P—K3   BxNch   11 B—K2   N—N3

After 12 B—N3, Castles; 13 Castles KR, White's two Bishops and slightly greater freedom of action give him the better prospects.

(b) 4 P—K4 Variation

1 P—Q4   N—KB3   3 PxP   N—N5
2 P—QB4   P—K4   4 P—K4   . . . .

Here White's objective is to develop rapidly. But he must be careful not to overextend himself.

| 4 .... | NxKP | 5 P—B4 | N—N3 |

Apparently better than 5 ... KN—B3, which leaves White with a much freer game after 6 P—QR3, P—QR4; 7 B—K3, N—R3; 8 N—KB3, B—B4; 9 Q—Q2, P—Q3; 10 N—B3, Castles; 11 B—Q3, BxB; 12 QxB, N—B4; 13 Castles QR.

132

(Position after 5 ... N—N3)

Black will attempt to prove that White's numerous Pawn moves have weakened his position.

| 6 B—K3 | .... |

If 6 N—KB3, B—N5ch; 7 N—B3, Q—B3!; 8 P—K5, Q—N3; 9 Q—Q3, P—Q3; 10 P—QR3, BxNch; 11 QxB, PxP; 12 NxP, NxN; 13 QxNch, Q—K3 with a level position.

| 6 .... | B—N5ch | 8 PxB | Q—K2 |
| 7 N—B3 | BxNch | 9 B—Q3 | P—KB4 |

White is hard put to it to defend the center.

| 10 Q—B2 | PxP | 12 BxN | P—Q4! |
| 11 BxP | NxP! | 13 PxP | B—B4 |

After 14 Castles, BxB; 15 Q—N3, N—Q2 Black's position seems somewhat exposed, but he just has time to castle and consolidate his position.

After 1 P—Q4, P—QB4 White can reply 2 PxP, but in that case Black recovers the Pawn comfortably with 2 . . . P—K3. The usual move against the counter gambit is therefore 2 P—Q5, which leads to a complex maneuvering game in which White has a greater command of the board.

1 P—Q4   P—QB4

An alternative line is 1 . . . N—KB3; 2 P—QB4, P—B4; 3 P—Q5, with this likely continuation: 3 . . . P—K3; 4 N—QB3, PxP; 5 PxP, P—Q3; 6 N—B3, P—KN3; 7 P—KN3, B—N2; 8 B—N2, Castles; 9 Castles, P—QR3 (in the hope of gaining space on the Queen-side with . . . P—QN4); 10 P—QR4!, QN—Q2; 11 N—Q2, KR—K1; 12 P—R5! with considerable pressure.

2 P—Q5   . . . .

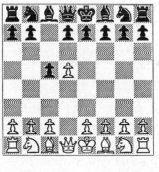

133

(Position after 2 P—Q5)

A position which leaves both sides with scope for considerable maneuvering. As a rule White has the better prospects because Black's position is apt to become cramped.

| 2 . . . . | P—K4 | 3 P—K4 | P—Q3 |
| | 4 B—Q3 | N—K2 | |

Black can also try 4 . . . P—QR3, but then 5 P—QR4! rules out the intended . . . P—QN4.

Here 5 . . . P—B4 opens up the game to White's advantage: 6 P—KB4!, BPxP; 7 BxP, N—Q2; 8 Castles, N—KB3; 9 QN—B3! and White's free, rapid development will tell in his favor.

On the other hand, 5 . . . P—QR3; 6 P—QR4!, N—N3; 7 N—R3!, B—K2; 8 N—QB4!, Castles; 9 Castles, N—Q2; 10 B—Q2, P—N3; 11 P—QB3, R—N1; 12 P—QN4! leaves White with a strong Queen-side initiative.

| 6 P—QB4 | B—N2 | 8 Castles | P—B4 |
| 7 QN—B3 | Castles | 9 P—B4! | QN—Q2 |

By now playing 10 N—N3! White maintains a strong initiative, for example 10 . . . KPxP; 11 BxP, N—K4; 12 PxP, NxB; 13 QxN, NxBP; 14 KN—K4! and White's lasting pressure on Black's weak Queen Pawn is embarrassing. White has two decisive threats in N—QN5 and P—KN4, leaving Black at a loss for a good continuation.

DUTCH DEFENSE

As in the Queen's Gambit Declined and the Queen's Indian Defense, Black fights for control of the King 5 square. In this defense he carries on the fight by playing an early . . . P—KB4. He can then continue the struggle with . . . P—Q4, or he can play . . . P—Q3 with a view to forming a counter-center with . . . P—K4.

Theorists are pretty well agreed that White's best course is to fianchetto his King Bishop, striking at the important center squares. The development of White's King Knight poses an interesting problem—to develop it to King Bishop 3, where it bears down on the King 5 square; or to play N—KR3 followed by N—KB4, to bear down on the Queen 5 square. Both methods have their good points.

(a) P—KN3 Variation

1 P—Q4	P—KB4	2 P—KN3	N—KB3
3 B—N2	P—K3		

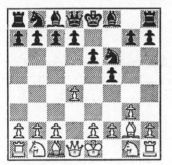

134

(Position after 3 . . . N—KB3)

White must choose between developing his King Knight at King Bishop 3 or King Rook 3.

4 N—KB3	....

We may consider this the main line, although 4 N—KR3 is an excellent alternative: 4 . . . P—Q4 (Black has a "Stonewall" formation); 5 Castles, B—Q3; 6 P—QB4, P—QB3. Then after 7 N—B3, QN—Q2; 8 Q—Q3, N—K5; 9 P—B3!, NxN; 10 PxN, White is ready to smash the center with P—K4.

Another alternative is 4 N—KR3, B—K2; 5 Castles, Castles; 6 P—QB4, P—Q3; 7 N—B3, Q—K1; 8 P—K4, PxP; 9 N—B4!, P—B3; 10 N/B3xP with a fine game for White.

4	B—K2	5 Castles	Castles
6 P—B4	P—Q3		

If Black adopts the Stonewall formation with 6 . . . P—Q4, White can get a clear positional advantage in several ways. For example 7 P—N3, P—B3; 8 B—QR3! By exchanging the black-squared Bishops, White leaves Black with the white-squared Queen Bishop, which is hemmed in by the Black Pawns on white squares.

Another way after 6 . . . P—Q4 is 7 P—N3, P—B3; 8 N—B3, Q—K1; 9 Q—B2, Q—R4; 10 N—K5, QN—Q2; 11 N—Q3!, P—KN4; 12 P—B3! with a view to P—K4! with a powerful initiative in the center.

| 7 N—B3 | Q—K1 | 8 R—K1 | . . . . |

A good alternative for White is 8 Q—B2, Q—R4; 9 B—N5, P—K4; 10 PxP, PxP; 11 BxN!, PxB; 12 N—Q5, B—Q1; 13.QR—Q1, P—B3; 14 N—B3, B—K3; 15 N—KR4! and White has all the play.

| 8 . . . . | Q—R4 |

Even after 8 . . . Q—N3 White can play 9 P—K4!, for after 9 . . . PxP; 10 NxP, NxN; 11 RxN, QxR?; 12 N—R4, Black's Queen is trapped.

| 9 P—K4 | PxP | 10 NxP | NxN |
| 11 RxN | . . . . | | |

White, with his superior development, has lasting pressure on Black's position.

1 P—Q4   P—KB4   2 P—K4   . . . .

A gambit attack which can give Black a great deal of trouble unless he plays carefully.

2 . . . .   PxP   3 N—QB3   N—KB3

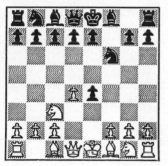

135

(Position after 3 . . . N—KB3)

After 4 B—KN5 Black must avoid the trap 4 . . . P—Q4? for after 5 BxN, KPxB; 6 Q—R5ch, P—KN3; 7 QxQP White comes out a Pawn ahead.

4 B—KN5   N—QB3!

Black can hold his own, for example 5 P—B3, P—K4!; 6 P—Q5, N—Q5; 7 PxP, B—K2; 8 B—QB4, P—Q3!; 9 KN—K2, N—N5!

Or 5 P—Q5, N—K4; 6 Q—Q4, N—B2; 7 BxN, KPxB; 8 NxP, P—KB4; 9 N—N3, P—KN3!; 10 P—KR4, B—R3!

These variations show how Black gets an excellent game by consistently developing and seeking counterplay.

MISCELLANEOUS CLOSE OPENINGS

From here to the end of the book we shall consider close openings which are for the most part not characterized by the move 1 P—Q4. They are given here to complete our survey of the most important close openings.

In only one case (the Catalan System) is P—Q4 played by White at an early stage. In the other lines, the double advance of a center Pawn is either delayed or altogether avoided by White.

For most players this is a novel state of affairs and a rather unpleasant one. The play strikes the uninitiated student as formless and groping, the future swathed in mystery. Yet such openings have their place in chess; and it is therefore useful to be familiar with their general outlines.

Finally, there is this point to be considered: You may not care to play such openings with the White pieces, but now and then you will find yourself on the Black side. If you are familiar in a general way with the underlying ideas and potentialities of each formation, you will be well equipped to meet the novel problems that such openings pose.

RETI OPENING

and Related Systems

Reti's Opening, starting with 1 N—KB3, has great flexibility and possibilities of transposing into many other openings. It involves, as a rule, the immediate fianchetto of White's King Bishop and the ensuing fianchetto of the remaining Bishop. White's strategy is to control the center squares from the flanks. Black generally counters with aggression in the center in order to obtain equality.

(a) London System

1 N—KB3	P—Q4

Black can fend off an immediate decision by first playing the flexible 1 . . . N—KB3, which may transpose into many other openings.

2 P—B4	P—QB3

Now White has the option of transposing into the Slav Defense (page 113).

3 P—QN3	N—B3		4 P—N3	B—B4!

A good development for this Bishop, which now bears strongly on the center.

5 B—KN2	QN—Q2		6 B—N2	P—K3
	7 Castles		. . . .	

136

(Position after 7 Castles)

Black is well on the way to achieving a model development and need not fear the coming struggle for the center.

7	P—KR3

In order to create a haven for his Queen Bishop. He can also continue his development directly, for example 7 . . . B—Q3; 8 P—Q4, Castles; 9 N—B3, Q—K2; 10 P—QR3, P—QR4!; 11 N—KR4, B—KN5 with an excellent position for Black.

8 P Q3	B K2	9 QN Q2	Castles

With Black's Queen Knight ready to go to Queen Bishop 4, he need not be afraid of White's P—K4, for example 10 Q—B2, B—R2; 11 P—K4, PxKP; 12 PxP, N—B4 with a good game for Black.

10 R—B1	P—QR4	12 R—B2	B—Q3
11 P—QR3	R—K1	13 Q—R1	Q—K2

Note how White bears down on the center from the wings. Black's game is playable.

(b) 2 ... P—Q5 Variation

1 N—KB3	P—Q4	2 P—B4	P—Q5

137
(Position after 2 . . . P—Q5)

According to "hypermodern" theory, Black has compromised his position by advancing the Queen Pawn. In actual practice, the Pawn has a cramping effect on White's game.

3 P—K3	N—QB3!	5 NxN	QxN
4 PxP	NxP	6 N—B3	B—N5!

Black has seized the initiative.

7 Q—R4ch	B—Q2!	9 B—K2	B—B3
8 Q—N3	Q—K4ch!	10 Castles	Castles

Black retains the initiative and has lasting pressure on White's backward Queen Pawn.

(c) King's Indian Reversed

1 N—KB3	N—KB3	2 P—KN3	P—KN3

White is playing the King's Indian Defense with a move in hand. If instead of the text Black plays 2 . . . P—Q4, a likely continuation is 3 B—N2, P—K3; 4 Castles, B—K2; 5 P—Q3, Castles; 6 QN—Q2, P—B4; 7 P—K4 with an excellent game for White.

3 B—N2	B—N2	4 Castles	Castles
	5 P—Q3	. . . .	

138

(Position after 5 P—Q3)

Black can still choose between an eventual . . . P—Q3 or . . . P—Q4.

5	P—Q4

Also after 5 . . . P—B4; 6 P—K4, N—B3; 7 QN—Q2, P—Q3; 8 P—QR4 followed by N—B4 White has an excellent game.

6 QN—Q2	P—B4		8 R—K1	P—K4
7 P—K4	N—B3		9 PxP	NxP

Now White continues 10 N—B4 with a good game.

CATALAN SYSTEM

This opening features the fianchetto of White's King Bishop (as in the Reti Opening) and P—Q4 (as in the Queen's Gambit). It abounds in positional finesses that can prove fatal for Black if he plays carelessly.

1 P—Q4	N—KB3		3 N—KB3	P—Q4
2 P—QB4	P—K3		4 P—KN3	....

139

(Position after 4 P—KN3)

This position can be reached by many transpositions, as for example 1 N—KB3, P—Q4; 2 P—B4, P—K3; 3 P—KN3, N—KB3; 4 P—Q4 etc.

4 . . . .   PxP

More interesting—and more complicated—is the alternative 4 . . . B—K2; 5 B—N2, Castles; 6 Castles, P—B4; 7 BPxP, NxP! (not 7 . . . KPxP leading into the inferior Tarrasch line—p. 111); 8 P—K4, N—N3; 9 N—B3, PxP; 10 NxP, N—B3; 11 NxN, PxN; 12 Q—K2, P—K4.

In this position White undoubtedly has possibilities of pressure against Black's weak Queen Bishop Pawn. On the other hand, Black's excellent development gives him ample resources.

5 Q—R4ch   B—Q2!

Simpler than 5 . . . QN—Q2; 6 QxBP, P—QR3; 7 B—N2, P—QN4; 8 Q—B6, QR—N1; 9 Castles, B—N2; 10 Q—B2, P—B4; 11 P—QR4, Q—N3 with a difficult position that gives both sides fighting chances.

6 QxBP   B—B3   7 B—N2   B—Q4

Black has countered White's fianchetto without weakening his position in any way. After 8 Q—B2, N—B3; 9 Q—Q1, B—N5ch—or 8 Q—Q3, P—B4; 9 N—B3, B—B3; 10 Castles, QN—Q2; 11 R—Q1, Q—N3 the position is even.

ENGLISH OPENING

After 1 P—QB4, Black has many replies, such as 1 . . .
N—KB3 or 1 . . . P—K3, which are likely to transpose into
other openings. Generally speaking, it is only 1 . . . P—K4
which gives this opening independent status. In the ensuing
play it is White's object to utilize 1 P—QB4 to control the
Queen 5 square. The logical way to do this is to fianchetto
the King Bishop, which is consequently one of the most popular positional motifs of this openings. Black must fight
energetically for control of the center in order to maintain
equality.

(a) King Fianchetto Variation with . . . P—Q4

1 P—QB4	P—K4	3 P—KN3	P—Q4
2 N—QB3	N—KB3	4 PxP	NxP
	5 B—N2	. . . .	

140

(Position after 5 B—N2)

*Note how powerfully White's fian-
chettoed King Bishop bears down on
the long diagonal, particularly on the
vital center square Queen 5. Black
must come to a decision about the
future of his attacked Knight.*

Black can maintain the Knight at his centralized post with
5 . . . B—K3, but after 6 N—B3, N—QB3; 7 Castles, B—
K2 White forces Black to give way with the dynamic 8 P—
Q4! Then, after 8 . . . PxP; 9 NxP, N/Q4xN; 10 PxN, NxN;

11 PxN, P—QB3; 12 R—N1! White still maintains his pressure on Black's game.

| 5 .... | N—N3 | 7 N—R3! | Castles |
| 6 P—Q3 | B—K2 | 8 Castles | N—B3 |

White's 7 N—R3 is a notable exception to the rule that it is poor play to develop a Knight to the side of the board. On King Rook 3 this Knight allows the Bishop to exert full sway on the long diagonal, and also permits the early line-clearing advance P—B4! (Both objectives would be blocked by the orthodox N—KB3.)

| 9 P—B4! | R—N1 | 10 PxP | NxP |
| | 11 N—B4! | .... | |

White's position is distinctly superior. His fianchettoed Bishop and both Knights control the crucial center square Queen 5; he has an open King Bishop file; and his center Pawns have great potential power in case of an eventual advance.

(b) King Fianchetto Variation with . . . P—Q3

| 1 P—QB4 | P—K4 | 3 P—KN3 | P—KN3 |
| 2 N—QB3 | N—QB3 | 4 B—N2 | B—N2 |

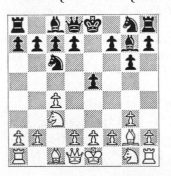

141

(Position after 4 . . . B—N2)

White has the best of both worlds: he not only controls the important Queen 5 square, but he can also control his own Queen 4 square with P—K3 and utilize this Pawn move to build a Pawn center.

5 P—K3!	P—Q3		8 NxP	NxN
6 KN—K2	KN—K2		9 PxN	Castles
7 P—Q4	PxP		10 Castles	N—B4

*After 11 P—Q5, R—K1; 12 N—K4!, P—KR3; 13 Q—
Q3! White has a very superior position, as he can increase
his positional advantage with R—N1 and B—Q2 followed by
B—QB3!*

(c) Four Knights' Variation

1 P—QB4	P—K4		3 N—B3	N—B3
2 N—QB3	N—KB3		4 P—Q4	....

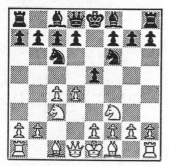

142

(Position after 4 P—Q4)

*White immediately opens up the posi-
tion on the theory that he can seize
the initiative, for example 4 . . . P—
K5; 5 N—Q2, NxP; 6 N/Q2xP, N—
K3; 7 P—KN3 with a promising position for White.*

4	PxP		7 B—R4	BxNch
5 NxP	B—N5		8 PxB	N—K4
6 B—N5	P—KR3		9 P—B4!	....

Much more vigorous than the routine 9 P—K3, N—N3;
10 B—N3, N—K5 with a good game for Black.

9 ....   N—N3

Not 9 . . . NxBP?; 10 P—K4!, N—K6; 11 Q—K2, NxB;
12 P—K5!, Castles; 13 N—B5! with a winning game.

| 10 BxN | QxB | 12 P—K4 | P—Q3 |
| 11 P—N3! | Castles | 13 B—N2 | P—B3 |

After 14 Castles, R—K1; 15 R—N1 White has consider-
ably more mobility, while Black has vague possibilities of
menacing White's weak Queen Bishop Pawns.

BIRD'S OPENING

A rare opening, as 1 P—KB4 contributes nothing to White's development. The idea of controlling the King 5 square often leads to a kind of Dutch Defense (p. 164) with colors reversed. Black has a number of ways to obtain an excellent game.

| 1 P—KB4 | N—KB3 |

From's Gambit (1 . . . P—K4) is not quite satisfactory, for example 2 PxP, P—Q3; 3 PxP, BxP; 4 N—KB3, P—KN4; 5 P—Q4, P—N5; 6 N—N5!, P—KB4; 7 P—K4!, P—KR3; 8 P—K5, B—K2; 9 N—KR3, PxN; 10 Q—R5ch, K—B1; 11 B—QB4, Q—K1; 12 QxP/R3 with a decisive attack in return for the sacrificed piece.

| 2 P—K3 | P—KN3 | 3 N—KB3 | . . . . |

Nor is the immediate Queen fianchetto very promising, for example 3 P—QN3, B—N2; 4 B—N2, P—Q3!; 5 Q—B1, Castles; 6 N—KB3, N—B3; 7 B—K2, B—N5; 8 Castles, P—K4! and Black has the better game.

| 3 . . . . | P—Q4 |

143

(Position after 3 . . . P—Q4)

White can now resort to a Stonewall formation, but after 4 P—Q4, B—N2; 5 B—Q3, Castles; 6 QN—Q2, P—B4; 7 P—B3, P—N3; 8 Q—K2, B—N2 Black has a fine game.

4 B—K2	B—N2
5 Castles	P—B4
6 P—Q3	N—B3

7 Q—K1	Castles
8 Q—R4	Q—B2
9 QN—Q2	P—K4

Black has an excellent game in this position (a Dutch Defense with colors reversed).

INDEX